JOSEPH F. KING

KAGAWA

Toyohiko Kagawa in His $1.85 Laborer's Garb

K A G A W A

by

William Axling

Harper & Brothers Publishers

NEW YORK AND LONDON

KAGAWA

Copyright, 1932, by
Harper & Brothers
Printed in the United States of America
TENTH EDITION
K-K

CONTENTS

FOREWORD

Toyohiko Kagawa still stands at the flood-tide of life. Richer and riper years lie in the womb of fas-future. It is too early to write his biography. The fascinating task of recording his whole life story the author bequeaths to an abler pen in some distant day.

But this flaming spirit—son of the mystic East—his message, bursting eruptive and glowing out of the depths of a great soul, and his adventurous life, fling out a ringing challenge to a world which has grown cold and cynical and is merely marking time.

Here is a figure who on the stage of our modern world not only speaks with the voice of a prophet, but translates into heroic living those principles and practices which through all ages have been dynamic with redemptive and creative influences.

There are two Kagawas. There is the Kagawa who has been aureoled and idealized by the fervent devotion of his friends and followers. There is also Kagawa the man of human clay fighting his way toward the heights.

The author has endeavored to present an unvarnished recital of Kagawa's twoscore and four years of life and work. He has plunged deep into Kagawa's voluminous writings and here and there has woven into the story utterances which open windows into his hidden life and reveal the workings of his mind and heart.

The paragraphs on the page opposite each new chapter, and those closing each chapter, as well as many of the paragraphs which appear in the body of the book set off with quotation marks, are translations from the Japanese made by the author from a series of two hundred meditations written by Dr. Kagawa for a Tokyo daily during those long dark days when he was threatened with total blindness. Later they were published in book form. All of the quotations in this volume, unless otherwise indicated, are translations from Dr. Kagawa's books or addresses published in Japanese. None of this source material has heretofore been translated into English.

There is an Oriental saying that "Light issues from the East." Out of the mystic, mature East, with its awakening consciousness of social solidarity, there flames a light which the West sorely needs. If this volume can serve as a torch, bearing this light westward, the author's highest hope will be realized.

The author wishes to acknowledge his indebtedness to Dr. and Mrs. Kagawa for their very helpful cooperation in making their personal files and other necessary source material available, to Mrs. Edna Linsley Gressitt, who read the first draft of the manuscript and made valuable suggestions, and to Mrs. Edith E. Bott for her interested and sympathetic stenographic services. Mrs. Axling also has rendered invaluable help as a counselor and friendly critic.

WILLIAM AXLING.

Tokyo, Japan
January, 1932

I

WHERE THE UNSEEN FORCES PLAY

THE MIRACLE OF ME

It is not necessary to go far afield in search for miracles. I am myself a miracle. My physical birth and my soul's existence are miracles. First and foremost the fact that I was ever born is a miracle. The fact that I am still alive despite my shadow-like, weakened body battling a host of devils of disease is a miracle.

Yet the greatest miracle of all is the reality of my soul. That I should be made victorious in temptations, be the object of God's care in a ruined world, be given assurance to go forward into the world of the devout, this is to me a master miracle. At times the storms of passion shake my soul to its depths, but a purer power, stronger a thousand times, has possession of my being and holds sway over me. When I think of this state of my soul it appears, even to me, a miracle.

To my heart, value immediately takes on reality and prayer erelong is reproduced in realization. In the depths of my soul I am daily conscious of the miracle of creation. The miracle of the resurrection becomes not a matter of yesterday, but takes place today in this soul of mine. A virgin conceiving and bearing God in her bosom becomes not an ancient tale in far-off Bethlehem but a present day fact within me.

—Kagawa's *Meditations*.

I

WHERE THE UNSEEN FORCES PLAY

MODERN MAN OUTLAWS MIRACLES. THEY FAIL TO FIT INTO his scientific rational interpretation of life and of the universe. But call it miracle, call it mystery, call it what you will, there is a strange mystic force that keeps creeping into the story of human life and works wonders along the way.

Toyohiko Kagawa thinks of himself as a miracle, and well he may. Heredity and environment are stubborn forces in the makeup of most men, but here is a man who in every respect is the antitype of all that characterized both his heredity and his environment. Like should beget like, yet in this instance uncontrolled passion brought forth an issue of purity, and gross materialism flowered into a flaming idealism.

Son of an unregenerate father, born out of wedlock, the unsought offspring of a dancing-girl, Kagawa's soul in the earliest dawn of its conscious life developed a passion for purity.

Reared in an atmosphere where sensuousness, selfishness, and self-indulgence held undisputed sway, the stripling of a boy rebelled against it all and courageously rebuked his guardian for his luxurious life, his unjust dealings with the tenants on his lands, and for his dishonesty in public life.

Taught from his earliest boyhood by precept and example that wealth, position, and power were life's goals, he early espoused poverty and came under the spell of a passion to serve.

Kagawa is right. His very birth was a miracle. According

to accepted moral standards he never should have been born. Humanly speaking, his birth was an accident, an unwanted by-product of unleashed passions.

Toyohiko Kagawa was born in Kobe, July 10, 1888. His father was a political figure of no mean dimensions. In his native province of Awa he was the headman of nineteen villages. Later the turn of the wheel of politics elevated him to the secretaryship of the Privy Council—the select group of men who served as advisers to the Emperor. This gave him the standing of a Cabinet Minister and brought him into intimate intercourse with many of the mighty men who made the Meiji Era—the "Era of Enlightened Reign."

Another turn of the wheel landed him in Kobe. This port city was feeling the thrill of Japan's newly established commerce with the outside world. Here he pioneered in the field of transportation. Like many a Samurai of that day who turned from the practiced arts of war and politics to the unknown ways of business, he failed in this venture.

Morally, the elder Kagawa was very much a man of his times. He left his wife to a lonely life in the country home at Awa while he made gay with wine and women. In the course of his revelings he took a special fancy to a geisha with light feet and lighter morals and installed her as one of his numerous concubines. Out of this illicit love four children were born. Toyohiko was one of these. He was a likely lad, and in order to make him his legitimate child the father went through the legal process of adopting him.

This life of lust was called upon to pay an early toll, and when Toyohiko had just passed his fourth birthday both his parents died. This proved a crisis in the life of the lad. He and an older sister were sent to the ancestral village home in Awa and intrusted to the care of the father's neglected wife and a foster grandmother.

These two elderly women lived a solitary, colorless life in a great thatched-roof house which straggled without plan or purpose hither and thither. Spacious rooms with thin tissue-paper doors and lattice windows and the floors covered with soft straw mats trailed one another in seemingly endless succession. Outhouses of every size and shape stood like silent sentinels in the surrounding yard. The whole establishment spoke in sad subdued tones of a glory that was no more.

In the Japanese garden to the rear, with its dwarf trees, red maples, and stone lanterns, some giant pines stood silhouetted against the sky. In the background huddled a grove of waving bamboo. Here and there were fruit trees that blossomed in the spring and bore great thick-skinned, yellow-shining oranges in the summer.

A stone's-throw away flowed the Yoshino River. As it hurried to its home in the sea, only five miles distant, it formed many a triangular sand dune along its course. A mile to the north the moat-inclosed Imperial mausoleum of one of the ancient emperors lifted its head above the surrounding fields.

The little lad, Toyohiko, found no welcome here. He was looked upon as an unwanted interloper. His stepmother left him coolly alone. Rarely did she speak to him. His foster grandmother, of whom he stood in deathly fear, put him to bed night after night with a volley of abuse. A bed-wetting habit brought down on him her unceasing wrath, and again and again his little body was tortured with the burning moxa to cure him of this fault. His guardians took turns in beating him whenever he failed to please their whims and fancies.

His elder sister, who accompanied him to this country home, was eccentric and hysterical and spent much of her time in tears in a back chamber. This led to permanent invalidism. She, too, showed him no love. They never played together. They never conversed in the familiar fashion that normally characterizes the relationship of brothers and sisters. This he attributes to the fact that she was forced to do the severest kind of physical labor and almost daily was beaten by her grandmother.

Whenever he saw his sister punished there surged up in his childish heart an intense hatred of life. At such times the grandmother's wrath leaped out toward Toyohiko as well, with the result that he was made a prisoner in one of the dark outhouses. The memory of his imprisonments at various times in all of these outbuildings has haunted him across the years. Love blasted before it bloomed and understanding hearts were utterly wanting in this home at Awa.

Brought up in such an atmosphere, the lonely lad made the bamboo grove, the Imperial mausoleum or the sand dunes along the river his rendezvous. Here as a wee lad he learned to commune with Nature in all her alluring moods. The time he dreaded most was the twilight hour when the booming of the temple bell summoned him to retrace his steps homeward. His arrival there meant a scolding, witnessing a quarrel, or the assignment of some unpleasant task.

Toyohiko entered primary school when he was but four years and nine months of age. The regulations require six full years, but his family being the wealthiest in the village, he seems to have been extended a special favor. The treatment accorded him at home branded his soul with the sense of being an outsider even at school. This complex robbed him of the courage to seek the friendship of the other children. This scion of aristocracy and wealth had, however, one fast friend prophetic of the course he would choose in after years. This companion was a classmate two years his senior, the son of one of the tenant farmers, who tilled the Kagawa lands and lived in a mud-plaster house contiguous to the main establishment. In the social scale Toyohiko and the poor landman's son were miles apart, but in the realm where soul meets soul they were the best of pals.

Out of school, as well, his being-an-intruder consciousness kept him from venturing forth to play with the boys of his neighborhood, although he eagerly joined them when invited. He spent most of the time with his books, hidden away in some secluded closet of the great dark house or lost in communion with nature's understanding, responsive heart.

Like all the promising boys of that time he was regularly sent to the Buddhist temple to study the Confucian Classics and to be drilled in the fundamentals of the Buddhist faith. From the Confucian Classics he learned the commanding place that filial piety and patriotic loyalty has in the thought-life of his people, and through the Buddhist teachings and its elaborate ritual there was nurtured in his boyish soul a sense of mystic awe and quiet reverence which has become habitual and controlling through the years.

Ability to read, however, threw open to him a new and fascinating world lying right within his reach. The family storehouse was a place of terror. Many hair-raising legends were gathered around its dark interior. Yet, boy-like, in spite of the fear which gripped at his heart, he one day made a daring excursion into its dim forbidden depths. The sights which greeted him thrilled his awakening mind. Here were stored mountain high all manner of ancient ancestral curios and historical relics connected with the office of the headman of the village. These dated far back to the Tokugawa period when Japanese knighthood was in its finest flower.

From huge armor-cases his eager hands brought forth suits of mail worn by those knights of war and chivalry. Long, age-scarred chests divulged fantastic garments and innumerable ceremonial costumes used by the Samurai long, long years ago. From other immense chests came beautiful swords of tested steel of every size and description. With consuming curiosity he drew each out of the scabbard-tomb to which peace had consigned it and gazed intently upon its shining blade. Many of these were of such enormous length that his boyish arms could scarcely handle them.

From bookcases came numberless books dating back to the Japanese Renaissance when the Chinese Classics were the rage among the élite. In corner closets he found pictures by famous masters depicting picturesque scenes of old Japan. Here were stored plum pickles which had been ripening for threescore years. The age of these delicacies simply staggered the lad's imagination.

Many were the half-days spent in browsing among the wonders of this treasure-house. Yet even these joyous hours were tinged with a stinging sense of loneliness. For fear of thieves, the contents of this storehouse were kept a profound family secret. Toyohiko was sternly forbidden to make known his discovery to any of the neighborhood boys. These journeys of adventure had to be made alone and this with many a pang pressed home to his child heart the extreme loneliness and abnormalcy of his life.

Whenever his foster-mother found it necessary to visit this storehouse she suddenly recognized his existence and summoned him to officiate as guide. She had an uncontrollable fear of the place and never entered it alone. She feared the dark. Moreover, there was a legend of age-long repetition that a white ghost periodically made its appearance in the house of Kagawa.

When guests came to this village home, however, the foster-mother and the grandmother made a dizzy change in the treatment of their charge. Then they masqueraded as angels of mercy. Toyohiko welcomed these intervals, for they were like the burst of a shaft of light into that dark and dreary dwelling.

The machine, with its mammoth factories and mass production, had not yet invaded Japan. Home industries supplied the nation's needs. The Kagawa establishment produced dye from the indigo plant and unrefined sugar from the sugar cane. At such seasons twenty to thirty people were employed. Moreover, merchants came from distant cities, and while canvassing the neighboring area for these products made the Kagawa house the center of their operations.

Love-starved Toyohiko helped with this work and sought eagerly among the workers and tradespeople for some one to befriend him. His grandmother oversaw and took an active part in all that was going on. In a busy mood she blustered about like a young hurricane, and while others were being tongue-lashed Toyohiko enjoyed a breathing spell.

Only when he reached the age of ten did his grandmother begin to address him as a human being. However, this was accompanied by many a word of scorn and curses poured out upon his real mother. Under their sting he hid himself and wept the bitterest of tears.

In lieu of a master of the house, he was, even at this tender age, sent on many an errand as a proxy for the family. The respect paid the headman of a township of villages was very great and the villagers accorded Toyohiko the treatment due a member of the headman's family. For this reason even when he attended the Buddhist mass he was ceremoniously ushered to an upper seat. This greatly bored and embarrassed the boy.

At the New-Year's ceremonies, when offerings were made before the ancestral shrine and the family partook of the festive rice and white wine, he was called upon to officiate as the man of the house. In the summer and fall he collected the rental from the peasants who tilled the Kagawa fields. At such times he took his seat behind a low desk and entered with a childlike scrawl the different accounts into the family ledger.

The family lived in the greatest simplicity. His grandmother begrudged him even a paltry cent for pocket money. On Buddhist festival days she salved her conscience by giving him a copper coin. With this he experienced the thrill of going to the temple and bargaining for some of the cheap trinkets for sale at that time, a clay figure, a toy looking-glass, or a charm with which to drive the demons away.

Toyohiko, like every child, had a fondness for sweets. To satisfy this craving he filled a tiny match-box with unrefined home-made sugar, another with bean flour, and stole away to the shadow of an outhouse or to the fields and feasted in secret. A sound scolding would have descended upon him had he chosen any other course.

He liked school and study, but was far more influenced by the farm work carried on on the Kagawa estate and in the village around him. In the summer-time, hip deep in the mud, he assisted in setting out, one by one, the tender rice plants in the slimy soil. Hour by hour he trod the monotonous waterwheel which lifted the water to higher levels and irrigated the paddy fields. Under the blistering summer sun he picked the fresh mulberry leaves to feed the silkworms and watched with tiptoe eagerness their miraculous transformation from wriggling larvæ to the delicate, glossy cocoons so essential to Japan's extensive silk culture.

In the fall he helped to harvest the rice, grown to golden ripeness, cutting it a fistful at a time with a short hand-sickle. During the winter he made sandals out of rice straw, helped to make salted pickles from great white radishes, and wove the rough home-spun garments which were universally worn by the farming folk at that time.

But his child mind and heart, his temperament and tastes, his whole budding personality, were more than anything else fashioned by Nature as she revealed herself in the fields, the plain, the moat, and along the banks and sand dunes of the river Yoshino. Here in her fairest form she exerted a subtle influence over the unfolding life of this lad and gave a set to his soul.

Often on a summer morning he was sent out on the plain to cut grass for the family horse. His frail body could scarcely carry the heavy hay basket. But he loved the horse and longed for one word of approval from his fault-finding guardians. Moreover, he was enchanted by the sweet fragrance exuded by the dew-covered grass as his short hand-sickle laid it low.

Winter and summer he fished in the river. All the year around he laid nets in the castle moat. A catch of shrimp was a joyous event. He became an adept at lobster-catching. Freedom from work on a summer day meant joyous play out in the open spaces. He caught butterflies, chased the dragonflies, hunted crabs, and made the animals his playmates. Nursing the babies of the skylark was his greatest joy. It was not easy to prepare food for these tiny pets, but it was fine fun. During all of his seven summers on the farm he was nursing mother to a brood of these embryo songsters of the sky. Chickens also were his care. When the little chicks fell sick he fed them medicated water and nursed them back to health. In miniature gardens of his own making he planted great stone jars which served as play places for his fish.

But tragedy trailed tragedy in the life of this lad. This time it came like a bolt from the blue. A neighbor child lay at the point of death and he was accused of having injured her. He rarely played with the neighborhood children. At school he made friends only with boys in the classes above him. There had been no opportunity to rowdy or quarrel with the wounded girl.

The false charge went like a sword-thrust into his sensitive soul. He felt that the villagers also considered him an intruder and bore the cruel accusation in the bitterness of his own bosom. In addition to the injustice of the false charge, he suffered the fear of being deprived of the honor he had won of being chosen the head of his class at school. For three days he wept without ceasing. A whole day he refused to touch food of any kind.

He had been permitted to start a savings fund from the sale of the eggs produced by his chickens. In this way he had accumulated the fabulous sum of five hundred coppers ($2.50). Innocent though he knew himself to be, he took all of this precious savings, gave it to the sick child, and sought the forgiveness of her parents. Even at this late date the wound inflicted by this experience remains unhealed.

Toyohiko's older brother, through profligate living, was laying waste the family fortune. In Japan, at the father's death, the eldest son becomes the head of the house. The problems of all the other members of the family must be referred to him for settlement. The elder brother's dissipation caused many a tear in that country home, but they were of no avail. The princely Kagawa estate was utterly wiped out by this son, who followed too closely in the steps of his sire.

Toyohiko, however, loved this brother, and on the occasions—once or twice a year—when he returned home, to fall asleep with his brother's arm around him was a never-to-be-forgotten experience. Driven to desperation by the false charge which had fallen upon him, he appealed to this brother for permission to leave the home which had lacked every vestige of home and the village which had branded him as a near kin to Cain.

When this child of Nature grew older he still responded to her mysterious moods, his was ever the understanding heart for all her various ways. He had discovered the way of approach to her which would prove most rewarding.

NOT ALL OF NATURE IS BEAUTIFUL. SHE CHANGES HER APPEARance according to the mood of those who approach her. To those stricken with sorrow the shining sun becomes an object of anathema. To those filled to overflowing with ecstasy even the foul water flowing sluggishly through the slums becomes a spring of exquisite bliss.

To those who have not developed the resources of the soul nature does not open her heart or unbosom herself. To the honest-hearted ancients the mountains and rivers appeared in the form of gods. To the men of the Middle Ages encaged in fear and apprehension nature was a den of demons.

To modern man, with his understanding of nature, it is for the first time possible to love nature as nature. Only he who has entered into the bosom of God can make nature his domain. The fact that there is a direct communion of spirit with spirit between the lily of the field and the poet is because love exists between them. Until abounding love comes upon the scene nature remains unborn. It may be said with truth that only he who loves the soul can deeply love nature.

—Kagawa's *Meditations.*

II

THE DARK THAT HERALDS THE DAWN

A LIBATION OF TEARS

A DIET OF TEARS IS NOT SAVORY. O SPIRIT OF MIDNIGHT, COLlect thou my tears in the bamboo tube. As my mass before God I will bring the tears of melancholy. I have now nothing else to offer on God's altar. Instead of the oil of the festival season I will bring before God my bamboo tube of tears. In it are stored tears of repentance, tears of gratitude for favors granted, tears in acknowledgment of blessings received, tears which flowed when emotions ran high, and tears of ecstasy. Created a child of tears, I am ashamed to advance into God's presence in the full light of day. Alone, in secret, in the midnight hour I seek His face.

Melt, O pupil of my eyes! Let their very lenses stream forth. Shall I not offer up to God the very marrow of my soul? I yearn that these tears for the altar shall emit the sweetest fragrance. I want them to be clear as crystal.

Tears! O tears! Tears wrung out of the soul's very marrow. Tears of ecstasy in drawing nigh to God! Tears of horror in not being able to enter into His presence. Tears which cause a plaintive melody as they alternate and intermingle! Come, O tears! Come without hesitation before God.

—KAGAWA'S *Meditations*.

II

THE DARK THAT HERALDS THE DAWN

THE MORNING OF KAGAWA'S LIFE DAWNED GRAY AND gloomy. After leaving the home at Awa he entered the Boys' Middle School at Tokushima, a large city on the island of Shikoku. In years he was a mere youth, but his tutelage in the school of pain at Awa and the lessons he had learned at Nature's knee gave him a wisdom far beyond his years. His prematurity made him the target for much bantering and laughter on the part of his fellow students.

He was appalled at the low moral tone of the dormitory and repelled by the conduct of the other boys. It soon became evident that his escape from Awa was not going to mean deliverance from loneliness. His mature ways and his refusal to run riot morally with the rest of the boys soon built a barrier between them and him. The greatest hardship, however, was being cut off from Nature—his loving foster-mother who had never failed to understand his every mood and minister to the deep-toned cry of his soul.

Lonely and alone, he increasingly surrendered himself to melancholy thinking. No day passed that his tears did not flow until his eyes grew weary and he could weep no more. Out of his agony he cries: "Life is like a raging wave. Even though you cut your way across the horizon, still the clouds roll on out beyond and the sky is far distant. Then the wind dies down and you are doomed to a life-horizon that is common and colorless.

"I have shouldered the cross of lofty principles and shining ideals, but when the dream of life ends will there be anything left but a cold corpse? I am denied even the hope of existence as a corpse. I will be reduced to ashes. Ashes the goal toward which I move! The thought of it drives me mad. When I think that those ashes will be beaten, driven by the rain and washed away into the gutter, a violent choking sensation sweeps over me.

"There is nothing to do but to drift with the clouds and be driven by the rain. Oh, that the thunders would roll and the rain descend in torrents! Or that the ship of life would suddenly sink and I could go down with it in peace."

Just at this critical stage missionaries came into his life. It was their hearts and homes that lifted the young Kagawa out of his slough of despair. Later two mission educational institutions trained him for his life work. Kagawa's first contact with Christianity was through Mr. Katayama, a Christian teacher in his school, but he points to Dr. H. W. Myers as his God-sent friend and father in the faith, and to Dr. C. A. Logan as his counselor and guide.

The latch-strings of the Myers and Logan homes in Tokushima were always out, challenging adventurous students to take a peep into a wider world. And where is the Japanese student who is not on tiptoe for such an adventure? They pulled them early and late.

There were good reasons for their crowding into these open doors. Here was a hearty welcome and an atmosphere of home for lonely lads away from home for the first time. Here was a friendly cup of tea and cakes and good things with foreign names and a taste that lingered. Better still, here was cheer. Here was music. Here was singing. Here was a break in the dull, colorless monotony of their school and dormitory life.

Here was an opportunity to try out English words and

phrases on good-natured, sure-enough users of that unusable language, and by their help to capture some new ones with which to astonish ones' fellows and teachers. Here was a chance to see first-hand how the men of the West lived and hear them tell of that world of wonder across the seven seas.

Above all here was teaching from a Book—a Book that sounded strange depths within themselves, depths of which they had never been conscious. A Book and a Personality speaking through that Book which taught them things their intuition and conscience affirmed must be true. Truths which brought new hope to their hearts, set their feet in a new path, and opened up vistas of a new and ever enlarging life.

Was it an accident, a mere chance, that the heavy-hearted youth from Awa joined the trek to these missionary homes? Or were the unseen, mystic forces again at work? Dr. and Mrs. Myers, as well as Dr. and Mrs. Logan, fathered and mothered him. Dr. Myers told him of a God who cares. He took him out under the open sky, turned his sad, tear-stained face toward the sun, and said, "Look at the sky, look at the sun, let your tears evaporate and then we will laugh." The miracle was wrought. Laugh they did. And Kagawa has been laughing ever since, though often it has been a symphony of laughter and tears.

"Consider the lilies, how they grow! they toil not, neither do they spin; yet I say unto you, that even Solomon in all his glory was not arrayed like one of these. But if God doth so clothe the grass in the field, which today is and tomorrow is cast into the oven, how much more shall he clothe you, O, ye of little faith?"

He read and reread it. He memorized the whole chapter. He knelt. The pent-up yearning of his heart burst into a poignant cry, "O God, make me like Christ!" a prayer and a dedication to an overmastering life purpose. The dawn broke. His spirit was flooded with light and life. His melancholy melted away like the mist before the rising sun. Kagawa was born again.

Life immediately took on a new meaning. He felt that he had been given a divine mandate to serve the poor. Reading of Canon Barnett, an Oxford professor, living in the slums, he eagerly dedicated himself to a life of poverty and set his feet in the thorny path of service. Hearing that the poor in Tokyo were living in hovels six feet square, he decided that he must live in no larger quarters.

Bitter opposition developed in the home of his wealthy uncle where he was staying, but joy welled up in his heart as he hid himself under the bedclothes and communed with God. His refusal to acquiesce to his uncle's demand that he renounce his new-found faith and purpose resulted in the ban of disinheritance falling upon him, and this scion of aristocracy and affluence was driven forth from under the roof of the proud Kagawa family, possessing nothing but the garments which he wore. Poverty was for him no longer a sentimental ideal, but a stark and stinging reality. He tasted the bitterness of its ways to the last dark dregs.

In 1905 he entered the Presbyterian College in Tokyo. He had read Kant's *Pure Reason* and Goethe's *Faust* in English before he graduated from the Middle School. On entering college he astonished his fellow students by reading such books as Kant's *Critique of Pure Reason*, Darwin's *Origin of Species*, Ruskin's *Modern Painters*, and Max Müller's *Sacred Books of the East*. They accused him of posing and not understanding what he read.

He had a perfect mania for books. During his two years'

stay in this institution he read practically all the important books in its library. His presence in the classes embarrassed some of the teachers because he had read more widely than they in many a field. The students called him, "The Transcendentalist" because of his interest in philosophy, social problems, and subjects beyond the thought range of his fellows. His interest swept the whole reach of human life.

Genius is a law unto itself and does not readily recognize authority. He presented a problem to his teachers. They found it difficult to standardize him and fit him into the hard and fast institutional pattern. He showed nonconformist tendencies. He had his own ideas and ideals and was militant in their defense. He "liked what he liked," with the result that he neglected subjects in which he was not interested and in many of the required studies stood low at the examinations.

He had an avaricious appetite for books, but he was even more avaricious for action and expression. A wide chasm yawns between the ideals and realities of most folk, but even during his student days Kagawa had a passion to practice. He rescued a castaway kitten out of the gutter and gave it a home in his room. He took pity on a homely deserted dog and adopted it as his charge. To the protest of the dormitory boys he replied, "Anyone will befriend a good-looking, healthy dog, but no one will care for an unfortunate cur like this unless I do it."

To cap the climax he shared his room with a beggar picked up by the wayside. The students were not slow in showing their resentment. They shunned him and his ragged room-mate. Kagawa, however, shared his food and his bed with him and treated him like a brother long lost.

He gave away his meager money allowance, his shoes, even the garments on his back, to beggars in distress, and wore rags himself. The women of the college church provided him with a new kimono, but it soon went the way of the rest. To needy students he gave his last copper and clothing that he himself sorely needed.

He fearlessly espoused unpopular causes and here on the threshold of his life showed an affinity for the prophets. Already he spoke a language that was strange to the standpatters and the worshipers of the god of things as they are. At this time the very word "socialism" was anathema in Japan. Yet at the meetings of the Students Literary Society he daringly advocated socialistic principles and practices.

As a result of reading Tolstoy he became an ardent believer in non-violence. The Russo-Japanese war was at its most critical stage. The tension throughout the Empire had reached the breaking-point. The one-hundred-percenters were combing the nation for spies and pacifists and railroading them to jail on any or no pretext. Nevertheless, openly and unafraid he urged his pacifistic views, opposed the war from the school platform, and brought down upon himself the wrath of the student body. They branded him as an upstart, a traitor, and ostracized him.

He would not, however, be silenced, and the students determined to take strong measures. Under cover of night they lured him to the college baseball-ground. Here twenty students, including some from the theological department, greeted him with shouts of "Pacifist!" "Betrayer!" and a shower of well-directed blows. Like Stephen of old, he simply folded his hands, quietly bowed his head to the blows, and lifted his voice in prayer: "Father, forgive them, for they know not what they do." From that group have come men who today are outstanding figures in the nation's life. One is a prominent pastor who some years later, when Kagawa was ordained to the Christian ministry, again laid hands upon him, this time to offer the ordination prayer.

All the while he was a flaming evangel. He rebuked Christians who had fallen into formal ways. In season and out of season he pleaded with men and women to get right with God and with their fellow men. His prayers in public and in private were watered with tears and burst like a pent-up flood out of his soul. In the end his fellow students were forced to acknowledge that he outprayed them, outloved them, outsacrificed them, and outlived them.

In the second year of his college career he was stricken with tuberculosis, the disease which terrorizes and devastates the youth of fair Japan. Hemorrhage followed hemorrhage. He was compelled to leave school and went to an isolated seashore village in search of health. Here for a whole year he had a rendezvous with death. In his weakened condition storms of doubts raged around him and his soul tasted the very agonies of hell. Though broken physically, he continued his reading and spent himself in acts of service and in an effort to evangelize the fishing-folk around him.

At the college in Tokyo and again out on the seashore between the attacks of hemorrhages he poured brain and heart into the writing of the first draft of a novel. This, his first fiction, which eventually singled him out as one of Japan's mightiest men with the pen, was written in such desperate poverty that he could not even buy paper on which to write. The whole tentative draft was written (with a Japanese writing-brush) over the printed pages of old castaway magazines.

Finally in his hand-to-hand wrestle with death he summoned all his powers of will and faith in one mighty effort to overcome, put the demon under his feet, and live. He had made only a partial recovery, but he gave up recuperating and entered the Kobe Theological Seminary to continue preparations for his life work.

While a student here a disagreement between two of the teachers resulted in the dismissal of one of them. Kagawa and four other students, feeling that the discharged teacher had been wronged, severely criticized the faculty for its action. This incident brought on a student strike.

The faculty looked upon Kagawa and the protesting students as the ringleaders and voted to expel them. This decision was announced at the chapel hour and the culprits were invited to go up and shake hands with the president as a parting ceremony.

Kagawa went forward, declared that he would not go through the sham of an empty handshake, and with tears streaming down his face gently stroked the president's hand, saying, "Christianity is a religion of love. A theological seminary must be a school of love. A school of love should guide a mistaken student. As God never abandons anyone, so a seminary ought never to drive a student away. Please forgive and reinstate the other four students and let the sentence of expulsion fall upon me alone." All were reinstated.

During his stay in this institution he showed again that he was made of unconquerable stuff. Disease still had him in its grip. Death still stalked him. But he had had it out with death. It no longer had any terrors for him. He spent his mornings studying, but his afternoons and evenings were devoted to preaching on the streets of Japan's most notorious slum. Shinkawa summoned him. He answered the call. His friends were alarmed at his rashness, but he declared that he would find his greatest satisfaction in dying in action.

To THOSE WHO KNOW GOD, PAIN IS THE SUPREMEST ART. IN order to enrich the stuff of our lives God has sown the earth with the seed of tears. Lovers of tragedy who pay a fee that they may weep over the third act in "The Forty-seven Ronin" should not fail to consider that there is meaning in the fact that without price God permits us to witness many an earthly tragedy. To those who live intensely pain is a puzzle test.

It is said that the lioness throws her whelp, born but three days, over the cliff. Those who are born of God must be as strong as God. Pain, misfortune, destitution, persecution, should not all of them be likened to the various jewels which adorn the crown of life?

I say to my soul, Let avalanches come! Let hurricanes roar! Let typhoons unite their forces and rage! Let earthquakes rock and rend! I fear none of them. To me pain is the highest of arts.

—KAGAWA'S *Meditations*.

III

A HEADER INTO THE SLUMS

ON FINDING GOD

God dwells among the lowliest of men. He sits on the dust-heap among the prison convicts. With the juvenile delinquents He stands at the door, begging bread. He throngs with the beggars at the place of alms. He is among the sick. He stands in line with the unemployed in front of the free employment bureaus.

Therefore, let him who would meet God visit the prison cell before going to the temple. Before he goes to church let him visit the hospital. Before he reads his Bible let him help the beggar standing at his door.

If he visits the prison after going to the temple, does he not by so much delay his meeting with God? If he goes first to the church and then to the hospital, does he not by so much postpone beholding God? If he fails to help the beggar at his door and indulges himself in Bible-reading, there is a danger lest God, who lives among the mean, will go elsewhere. In truth he who forgets the unemployed forgets God.

—Kagawa's *Meditations.*

III

A HEADER INTO THE SLUMS

FROM THE TIME THAT MODERN INDUSTRIALISM INVADED Japan the slums have been the festering sores of her large cities. The police knew of and accepted their existence. The criminal class made them its rendezvous. The prostitute quarters combed them for recruits. Occasionally an adventurous reporter made an excursion thither and came back with some gruesome tale which no one believed. Peasant folk were directed there in their search for a wayward son or daughter. To the people as a whole they were an unknown land.

Kagawa took his friends by sudden surprise when at the age of twenty-one he took a straight header into the depths of the Shinkawa slums. Here ten thousand people were sardined into houses six feet square, more like prison cells than homes. Often such a house had to accommodate a family of five or two families of nine to ten persons.

There were no windows. Light and air stole in through the open door. One community kitchen, a water hydrant, and a common toilet served the needs of a score of families. These houses faced upon unpaved alleys three to six feet wide. These alleyways reeked with filth; refuse from the houses, overflow from the toilets, and the backwash of overworked sewers.

As to occupation, these people were scavangers, freight-handlers, day laborers, factory workers, jinrikisha-pullers, basket-makers, tub-menders, boatmen, road workers, smoking-pipe menders, charcoal-ball makers, waste-paper collectors, venders of cheap sweets, cargo-carriers, fortune-tellers, gamblers, beggars, thieves, murderers, pimps, and prostitutes. Their income averaged from twenty-five to fifty cents a day when work was available, but much time was spent in enforced idleness.

The district swarmed with under-nourished children, covered from head to foot with scrofula and various kinds of skin diseases. Infant mortality reached the staggering height of over 500 in 1,000 as against 380 in other parts of the Empire.

Day and night, disease of every description did its deadly work all over this area. Under the veil of night crime and unseemly sin stalked unashamed through the dark alleys and in and out of the squalid hovels which passed for homes.

When once the young Kagawa found himself in the slums the desire to give his life for the under-privileged, which had been taking root in his soul for many a month, burst into a full-blown life purpose. Persecuted and threatened, he stood unmoved. He feared neither man, vermin, filth, nor disease. The itch, the pest, tuberculosis, syphilis—he lived, slept, and moved among them. He had made up his mind that his life-span was to be short at the best, and faced it all without anxiety or fear.

Here was an opportunity to act out the Sermon on the Mount on one of the most needy and most strategic stages of history, and that matchless Magna Charta of the larger life with all its challenging implications did not terrify him. He gloried in the belief that Christianity is not a religion of sensible men, but of men gone mad with love for God and man.

Christmas, 1909, stands out as a red-letter day in Kagawa's colorful life. On that day he carted his few belongings, with his own hands, from the seminary dormitory, and alone and unheralded made his way to the slums. The walls and ceiling of the hut in which he settled fairly screamed with blood and violence. Murder had been committed there, and even the red-handed murder-minded denizens of Shinkawa shunned it. It was reputed to be haunted and had stood tenantless since the night of that dark deed.

A business depression had the nation in its throes and the slums teemed with the poorest of the poor, who besieged him for a meal or a place to sleep. To give a night's lodging meant sharing his own bed and bedding, but he never refused.

His first applicant was a son of poverty suffering from a serious case of contagious itch. The adventurous savior of the slums looked at him covered from head to foot with itch blotches. "This is God testing me," he thought, and gladly made him his bedfellow. In due time he too was initiated into Shinkawa's Society of Scratchers.

Others there were who came to stay not for a night only but for a season. His first long-time lodger was a starved slave to drink. He labeled him the "Copper Statue" because of the color of his alcohol-soaked skin and the fact that he moved only under the greatest compulsion.

Another was a murderer and a jailbird who, haunted by the ghost of his victim, passed his days in fear and his nights in sleepless terror. He pleaded for the privilege of sleeping with Kagawa, believing that Kagawa's God would drive away his ghost. Night after night he fell asleep clinging desperately to his protector's hand. To lose hold of that reassuring grip in his sleep meant a sudden leap into the most terrifying of nightmares from which he was with difficulty aroused. For four long years and more every night this experience was repeated over and over.

The plea of an empty stomach and the statement that

for days he had lived on a diet of water opened the way for a third boarder. This ally of the poor now had four to feed. His total income was a monthly scholarship of $5.50, received from the Theological Seminary. This proved insufficient. He secured work cleaning chimneys. This brought in another $5 a month.

However, even $10.50 would not feed four hungry men. They met the emergency by diluting their rice with a liberal supply of water and reducing their meals to two a day. This two-meal-a-day rice-and-water-gruel diet continued for fifty days, when a gift of $2.50 from a friend provided them once more with a full meal.

At one time over ten down-and-outs were under his hospitable six by six roof. It became inadequate and they removed some of the walls in order to make room for all to lie down. Among them, one was in the last stages of tuberculosis, whose soiled, germ-infected garments Kagawa washed with his own hands. One was mentally deranged and, though well educated, was deserted by both family and friends. Another was a sick prostitute rotten with syphilis. It was through sharing his bed with a beggar that Kagawa contracted trachoma, the dread eye disease which has almost robbed him of his sight.

Some of the people believed that he was a rich man's son who had chosen to come to the slums to spend his money. Others thought that because he was a Christian he was receiving unlimited funds from foreign lands. They, therefore, considered it their right to inflict themselves upon him.

A beggar asked him for his shirt, saying "You pose as a Christian; failure to give it will prove you a fraud." He got the shirt. The next day he returned and demanded his coat and trousers. He got them as well. This left Kagawa with nothing to wear but a woman's kimono with a flaming red lining, the gift of a destitute but sympathetic neighbor woman. That woman's kimono with its tell-tale lining made him the butt of many a merry jest and much mirth everywhere he went.

Word got out that he had been intrusted with a sum of money to use for the very poor. A gambler chief appeared, pistol in hand, and demanded $15 of that money. Kagawa took to his heels and fled. His visitor fired five bullets into the wall of the room and instructed the "Copper Statue" to tell his benefactor on his return that every one of those five bullets meant business. In Shinkawa a gambler who had lost, and needed funds to retrieve his luck, was like a tigress robbed of her young. Anyone with money was legitimate prey. Kagawa decided that his life was worth $7.50 and a compromise was reached on that basis.

Gambling was a mania in Shinkawa. Men gambled away not only the last cent in their pockets, but the shirts on their backs. Children were sent to school or to their work in the factory in rags, and weeping bitter tears because their mothers had pawned their clothing while gambling. The highest ambition of the girls of the district was to marry a gambler, because it meant food, clothes, and money. The police were helpless. A raid on a game or a gambling-den was like an attempt to drive the flies from a decaying carcass. Moreover, interference was dangerous. A dagger or a pistol was as much a part of a gambler's outfit as the cards and the dice. And they were freely and fiercely used when a quarrel arose over the stake or when some one interfered with a game.

Illicit prostitutes swarmed in these alley-like streets at all hours, both day and night. Among them were wives, mothers of families, women on the verge of childbirth, and even thirteen-year-old children. The houses contiguous to Kagawa's hut were the center of their operations. They flaunted their damning trade in his face. They brazenly entered his home when he was in the midst of a passionate gospel plea and enticed away the young men in his audience.

Moreover the ruffians and bullies who took refuge here because of the powerlessness of the police made life miserable for this Christian idealist who had set out to redeem the slums. Their presence made him live daily under a drawn dagger.

They thought nothing of committing murder. On the contrary, many were proud of their murder record. It was a badge of distinction. For them prowess in murdering was the mark of a man. The more cases he could boast of, the greater man he felt himself to be. Furthermore, in the eyes of his fellows the halo of heroism grew in proportion as the number of victims increased. Some of them came bearing as tokens of honor the skulls of those whom they had assisted across the river Styx.

Knowing that Kagawa was a Christian, a non-resister, and that he never appealed to the police for protection, they plagued him with peremptory demands for money. When these demands were refused, out flashed a dagger or a kitchen knife. Many were the times that he was put to flight with one of these ruffians in swift pursuit, brandishing a vicious weapon. One of them attempted to play the rôle of a penitent, but when Kagawa saw through the sham and refused him money, a death-bearing stone was hurled at him. Another knocked out four of his front teeth.

On one occasion when this gospeler was pouring out his heart in a message on the street, a bully appeared, carrying a club. "A Christian priest! I hate them! Get out of here; you're blocking the traffic!" he shouted. For a moment the preacher acted as though he would meet force with force. This whetted the ruffian's longing for a fight. Suddenly, however, Kagawa took to his heels and ran, with the ruffian jeering and the crowd laughing. But the next day he was back and at it again.

Many of these bullies were pimps or masters of the unregistered prostitutes of Shinkawa, and when, as a result of Kagawa's attack on prostitution in his street preaching, a number of these women repented and turned from their wayward way, the storm broke. One appeared while Kagawa was eating, accused him of stealing his property, and smashed all the dishes on his table. Another who was making the wives of eleven men his concubines threatened him with a pistol. Another, the parent of a secret prostitute, threatened him with a kitchen knife. Still another, who had forced his own wife into prostitution, attacked him as a disturber of family relations!

One of these ruffians, overhearing Kagawa pray for help to forgive even enemies, jumped to the conclusion that he was the man, flew into a rage, kicked over a brazier of red-hot coals upon the straw mats of the meeting-room, and challenged the pray-er to let his God take care of them. When Kagawa scrambled to pick up the burning coals he tried to turn the laugh on him by shouting: "Your god is a joke! He makes you save yourself."

These bullies not only threatened and attacked Kagawa personally, but they broke the windows of his hut, smashed the few articles of furniture that it contained, and stole his cooking-utensils. But he never hit back. Had he done so, his career in Shinkawa would have come to an abrupt end. He either fled or smiled, whichever seemed the better strategy. If he fled, he soon returned and carried on as though nothing had happened.

Life was less than cheap in this slum; it was valueless. Murder was a common occurrence. The murder in the house occupied by Kagawa had been caused by a quarrel over ten cents. His first year in Shinkawa witnessed seven cases in his immediate neighborhood. A quarrel over a chicken head caused one of these. A wrangle in which two men claimed the same woman as wife caused another. A child of thirteen killed another of the same age. A mediator in a quarrel paid for it with his life. A priest lost his life when he refused to reveal to a ruffian the location of a gambler's den.

On holidays and festival days all Shinkawa held high carnival. Drinking was a major curse among these people, and on these days all who could get drink went on a wild spree. A drunken brain bred a spirit of discord and violence. On one New-Year's morning from five o'clock until nine Kagawa counted nineteen quarrels—family quarrels, gamblers' quarrels, quarrels over women, quarrels between women, and drunken brawls. In the course of such a day blood flowed freely, and ere it had passed the cry of "murder" had been raised.

The widespread practice of adopting infants and slowly starving them to death brought unspeakable agony to Kagawa's sensitive soul. There was a regular traffic in tiny tots so circumstanced, and because of the business depression this traffic was then at its height.

Unwanted babies were brought to middle-men, who bargained to take them at the rate of $15 plus ten garments for each child. They in turn sold them to traffickers in infants, who received $10 of this money and five of the garments. The family that finally adopted the child did so not because they wanted the child, but in order to get the $2.50 in money and the two garments which came with it as compensation for raising it. Many families made a business of adopting children and through starvation and mistreatment hastening them to an early death. Shinkawa had two hundred children who had come there through this system of adoption.

Kagawa, while still a theological student and unmarried, was himself driven to adopt such a tot in order to snatch it out of the jaws of death. An old woman was under arrest for maltreating an adopted infant. He rushed to the police station and found the child near death's door. It was examination time at the seminary, but he carried it back to his hut. Months of ill-treatment had reduced it to skin and bones. It had bowel trouble and ran a high fever.

That night he went to sleep fondling the tiny life which had been thrown into his arms and heart. During the days that followed he was busy with his infant charge rather than with preparations for his examinations. He tended it with tears. He fed it. He nursed it. He changed its soiled garments and washed them with his own hands. He gave it a new life and a new chance. He coaxed it back to health and happiness. He mothered it until he found a mother for it.

Bleary-eyed men, pistol-toting bullies, diseased prostitutes, skin-diseased juvenile criminals, half-naked women, and undernourished children threw the lurid conditions of Shinkawa into high relief. There was, nevertheless, another side to the picture. Here were people who, moved by their own bitter experience, readily gave their all to help a friend in need—women who in cases of illness came and offered their very last handful of rice; men who turned from urgent tasks to help a fallen comrade.

Underneath the rough exterior there ran a lot of the milk of human kindness. Back of their poverty and uncouthness there was a hidden bond of understanding and brotherhood which helped them over many a hard, rocky place in the road. Above all, the children with their unspoiled souls captured the heart of this Christian knight-errant who had sallied forth to fight the battles of beaten and broken humanity.

Kagawa put the drive of a great heart into the work of picking brands out of the fire. He conquered through love, but it was no easy victory. Love's victories are never cheaply won. They are secured at a fearful price. Christ conquered only through the Cross. His envoy in Shinkawa looked upon privations, insults, and attacks as mere incidents of the day's work. Others looked upon these people as alley spawn, a breed of the underworld. He looked upon them as folk. He loved them. He saw hidden in each one a priceless soul and a potential personality.

His day began with a six-o'clock street meeting at an open place where the people congregated before scattering for the day. This is a typical scene. A tubercular cough has its clutch on him. Yet he stands in a driving rain until drenched, and cries: "God is love! I will proclaim this until I fall. God is love! I do not mean that the unseen God is love. Where love is, there is God." Then he falls exhausted to the ground and rough but sympathetic hands carry him to his hut.

In Shinkawa babies were born without expense, but it cost $2.50 to bury them. No family could raise that amount and a death was a major calamity. Their problem was not how to have their children well born, but how to have them well buried.

Mother-love, father-love, knows no distinction of class, color, or circumstance. This love was not entirely lacking even in Shinkawa and parents wanted their babies decently buried—in a coffin and in a cemetery—but both cost money. They therefore brought their dead babies to Kagawa and begged him to bury them. During his first year he buried fourteen. In 1911 he provided Christian burials for nineteen babies. This is typical of what happened every year during his almost fifteen years of life in these slums.

He visited the sick. He comforted the sorrowing. He fed the hungry. He lodged the homeless. He became elder brother to the prostitutes, visiting them when they were ill and providing them with medicines. Even for the bullies he had a brother's heart and never lost an opportunity to put God's love into action in his dealings with them.

Parents turned to him for advice. Young people brought him their tangled life problems. Criminals made him their father-confessor. Sick prostitutes sought shelter under his roof and he cared for them. The children swarmed around him in such numbers that he was compelled to move his Sunday school to a vacant lot and hold the sessions out under the open sky.

He enlarged his working center by adding a room which served as a dispensary and hospital, and another which was crowded with routed and wrecked men and women. He himself continued to live in his six-by-six room. The ceiling was covered with newspapers to prevent a rain of dust. The walls were of mud. The straw-covered mats were so infested with vermin that they fairly heaved, and in the summer he had to construct a hammock bed in order to secure a minimum of sleep. They invaded even this.

Out of his own experience of deep distress he was able to reveal his strong soul to the storm-tossed lives around him and satisfy his passion for showing God's love to those for whom no one cared. His perilous pilgrimage into the slums enabled him to marshal into play all the forces of his versatile personality and to bring the impact of recreative life upon this human waste-heap.

He also proved himself a master with the pen. The fiction which he had written as a student while fighting for his life with tuberculosis lay buried beneath a pile of books and magazines. The publisher of the influential monthly *Kaizo* (*Reconstruction*) called at the slum hut one day in search of feature material for his publication. Kagawa brought forth his all-but-forgotten manuscript. The publisher read it, recognized in it the spark of genius, and urged that it be revised and released at once. Moreover, to the author's utter amazement, this keen judge of values in the field of fiction offered to purchase the manuscript for the then fabulous sum of $1,250.

Kagawa revamped it, put into the title and contents the story of his combat with death and his experiences in Shinkawa, and gave it to the reading world. It was first published as a serial, but attracted little attention. Later, however, when put out in book form under the title, *Across the Death Line*, the nation redeemed itself by buying up edition after edition. In an incredibly short time 250,000 copies were sold. This recognition put the young penman in the front ranks of the nation's writers.

His second book, *The Psychology of Poverty*, was a serious study of the causes and cure of poverty. He wrote a *Life of Christ* for children. He showed his versatility by publishing at the same time a book of poems and a dissertation on economics.

I AM FOND OF MEN. THE WORST, MOST FEAR-INSPIRING, DEmonized murderer somewhere in his make-up has that which is irresistible. Plagued by them, I flee. Often I left the slums of Shinkawa for a season because bullies made life a torture for me. Yet I did not abandon those rogues of the slums.

Nature is fascinating, but the children of the slums also

abound in interest. If I am privileged to play with them I will not say that nature surpasses them in attractiveness.

Sin makes men base. If there was no liquor and no syphilis the worst of rogues would inspire no fear. The rogue himself is not to be feared, but loaded with liquor he creates terror.

I cannot say that a man minus a nose because of the inroads of self-inflicted disease, or the stooped and broken courtesan, is more beautiful than a flower, but I cannot abandon hope regarding either of them. I cling to men. I love them. I can't help loving them. Even though I am cornered and forced to flee from men whom the demon of drink transforms into beasts, yet I speedily seek them out again when they return to a sober state.

—KAGAWA'S *Meditations.*

IV

IN THE RÔLE OF AN EMANCIPATOR

RELIGION FOR THE WHOLE OF LIFE

Some people say that social and religious movements are two different things. This, however, is said by those who fail to think of religion as an art concerned with the whole of life. If the material and the spiritual are separate entities, and if there is no relation between God and the world, this contention might be true. To him, however, who makes life the realization of the supremest good it is impossible to separate social and religious effort.

If religion is the whole life in action, how can social movements alone exist apart from religion? It is only the timid who interpret God and the world as a dualism. Until even the Stock Exchange is filled to saturation with God there is little hope for genuine religion.

—Kagawa's *Meditations.*

IV

IN THE RÔLE OF AN EMANCIPATOR

THE LOVE OF CHRIST AND A PASSION TO BEFRIEND THE POOR and make Jesus' way of life a solvent of the problem of poverty, led Kagawa to dedicate his life to the slums. But he never lost his passion for books. He never ceased to be a student. The most conspicuous furniture in his Shinkawa hut was a stack of shelves constructed out of the rough wooden cases in which gasoline-cans are packed for shipping. These shelves contained a marvelous library. Here were books that are everywhere recognized as authorities in the field of religion, poetry, philosophy, psychology, pedagogy, biology, economics, the social sciences, and the problems of labor.

Early in his career in the slums he declared: "The slums are a laboratory of life and of human society. From one point of view I am doing research work with the slum as my laboratory and man as my major. Some people think of me as administering palliative remedies, but I am an industrious scientist. I am researching life at one of its outbreakings in the social order."

He was not satisfied to be simply a mender of men. His experience in Shinkawa convinced him that the problem of the slums could never be solved in that way. He therefore turned the slum into a great laboratory for social research. He traced poverty to its source, studied its causes and effects, probed into contributory causes, and endeavored to discover the cure. Out of this study was born Kagawa, the Christian Socialist, the champion of the under-privileged classes, the daring labor leader and the consistent and persistent critic and foe of the present capitalistic, acquisitive social and economic order.

His study led him to the conviction that poverty had its roots in the labor situation. In the system of home industries and handcraft which characterized ancient Japan the employee was treated as a human being. He shared the employer's family life. The employer and employee ate at the same table, worked in the same room, and joined mind and hands in the same task. The human element entered into all their relations. They faced each other as man to man. They knew each other. They understood each other. Often the employer was moved by a parental interest in those who worked under his immediate oversight. Withal there was ample opportunity for creative work.

Modern industrialism, with its monster factories, its high-powered machines, its mass production, and the stranger-relationship between employer and employee, had changed all this, except that the rights were still all on the side of the employer and the laborer had no choice or voice as to the work he should do, the conditions under which he should work, the hours he should work, or the wages he should receive.

This was before the day of either the International Labor Bureau at Geneva or the present factory legislation in Japan. The employer needed only to cater to the stockholder and his insatiable hunger for big dividends. In many cases working conditions were a scandal. Hours were long. Wages were low.

Kagawa, the student, discovered that many of the ills which afflicted Shinkawa harked directly back to these labor conditions. He found a direct relation between the rate of infant mortality and the parents' wages. Where the income was low the death rate was high, and *vice versa.* Because of insufficient income half of the children were undernourished and died before they reached the age of five.

He found that the chief causes of tuberculosis and the other diseases which played havoc with life in this slum were undernourishment and long working-hours. He found that those about him resorted to drink in order to paralyze their brains and nerves and forget their suffering. Irritated by their lot, they sought a stimulant to ease the strain.

Moreover, poverty was the handmaid of the prostitution that polluted the slum. He witnessed a woman approaching her birth throes suddenly turn courtesan. Investigation revealed the fact that her husband was injured and ill and the family income cut off. He offered to tide them over until a better day, but it was too late. She had tasted of the street-walker's life and no longer desired to reform. She kept it up and forced an abortion.

Pondering on the unnaturalness of it all, he says, "Humanity by rights should not degenerate to such a state. If it comes to this it would be far better for them to be dancing, crying monkeys among the island forests in the South Seas.

"They did not drop to this depth of their own desire. They cannot eat without working. And working with their hands brings in but a pittance of ten or fifteen cents a day. On this they must live. To throw their chastity on the market means money without toil. For a simple-minded, unlettered woman this plan seems simple. Facing starvation, she barters her soul and discovers a means of livelihood. And once this life is entered, she cannot cleanse her soul and return again to her first chaste state."

Kagawa found himself playing the lonely rôle of a pioneer in his attack on the problem of the slum in Japan. There were no precedents to follow, no guideposts to point the way. In every phase of the work he was compelled to blaze new trails. He was young in years and eager to learn from the experience and experiments of others who had wrought effectively in this field. He therefore sought an early opportunity to go abroad for special study and first-hand observation. In 1914 the way opened and he set sail for America.

During the more than two years that he was absent from Japan, studying at Princeton University and investigating social service institutions in America, three of the girls in his Sunday school, whom he had baptized, were sold to houses of prostitution. Thirty of the boys whom he had brothered, overcome by the influence of their homes and their environment, became protégés of pickpockets and were sent to jail.

Mourning the fate of these who had been plucked out of the fold he cries: "Who stole those thirty-three precious souls? Bring them back! Bring them back! Bring them back once more to my breast! The present evil order has stolen those whom I so dearly loved and is killing them alive. It is like putting an oar into a stormy sea—every gain is followed by a backward swing."

He determined that the liberation of the laborer was the only way to save the slums. Impelled by a sense of divine call and a deep emotional drive, he set out to play the rôle of an emancipator. There were then 2,400,000 on Japan's labor roll. Their number has since jumped to 9,430,000: 5,280,000 free laborers and factory workers, 1,033,000 engaged in transportation, 1,158,000 working on roads and public works, 1,500,000 fishing-folk, and 459,-000 miners.

Kagawa's leap into the leadership of Japan's laboring-folk was fraught with dramatic significance. These toilers had been slowly coming to a consciousness of their worth and latent power. The ferment of social unrest and discontent had long been at work. The rumbling of a coming storm could clearly be heard in their ranks. But they lacked a leader, one who not only sensed their wrongs, but whose personality could dramatize their cause and command the sympathy of the nation.

Kagawa was the man for the hour. He had lived with them. He had suffered with them. He had wept with them. He knew them better than they knew themselves. Their cause was his cause. Their battle was his battle.

Moreover, his life in Shinkawa and his novel, *Across the Death Line*, which everyone was reading at the time when he stepped into the arena as the champion of the working-folk, focused every eye on them and their cause. They jumped with one spring right into the center of the national stage.

Some years previous Mr. Bunji Suzuki and others had organized in Tokyo the Yuai Kai (Laborers Benefit Society). As an evolution of this society Kagawa had helped to form the Japan Federation of Labor and organized the laborers of his area into a branch of this organization.

A contemporary writing at this time says, "If Suzuki is the father of the labor movement in Japan, Kagawa is the mother—his heart, his soul, his sympathy, his understanding of the laborers are like that of a mother—a wise mother."

The first outward evidence of the workers' growing consciousness of their place and power came in 1921 when the laborers of the Kawasaki and Mitsubishi Dockyards in Kobe went on a strike. They were the poverty-stricken workers whom he had befriended and to whom he had preached in connection with his work in Shinkawa. They turned to him. "Follow Kagawa!" cried 30,000 voices. He accepted the challenge and flung himself into the fight.

In order to keep the lid on labor the police had issued

regulations making it unlawful for laborers to form associations. In the interest of strategy and in order to control the strikers Kagawa found it necessary to organize them. He, therefore, disregarded the decree and organized the striking workers into a full-fledged labor union—the first one in Japan.

It was not a question of hours or wages, though the hours were long and the wages low. The strikers demanded the recognition of the labor union, its right to negotiate and the right to have a workers' committee in the factory. This meant that leaders would emerge from among the workers. They would then have a say in regard to such questions as hours, wages, and working conditions. It was an unprecedented demand and the employers fought it bitterly.

The strikers issued a manifesto to the nation. This, too, was an unheard-of procedure. "Laborers are personalities. They are not commodities to be bought and sold according to a scale of wages based on the market price. Furthermore, they must be given the right to organize. For this reason we who belong to the army of producers make the following proclamation:

"We are not machines. In order to develop our own individualities, to personalize society, and to secure a social order which will provide the producers a real culture and give them security as to their livelihood, we demand the right to regulate our own circumstances."

Kagawa opposed the use of violence and destructive tactics. At first only peaceful methods were employed, but the calling out of soldiers and the use of force on the part of the police stirred up the ire of the workers. The situation developed into a siege, with feeling running rampant on both sides.

The 30,000 laborers put their destiny in Kagawa's hands.

He planned and directed their campaign. He spoke to them *en masse* daily and kept up their morale. He took their demands to the dock authorities and in person pleaded their cause. One who saw him in action says, "When he stands as the leader of labor and gives battle for the blue-dressed hosts, one cannot but be impressed with his warrior-like spirit which flames to high heaven."

The police blacklisted him, called him an agitator, and buzzed around his hut in Shinkawa like bees around a swarming hive. Detectives tracked his every step. Finally they raided the headquarters of the strikers and placed him under arrest. One of the police, in arresting him, tore his clothing and beat him with a saber. He was handcuffed and dragged hatless and shoeless to the police station.

The judge, however, was considerate in his attitude and the prison-warden manifested all the leniency possible. The guards also treated him kindly. Kagawa called them brothers and showed neither temper nor resentment. His fellow prisoners treated him as a hero. Fearing that his presence among the admiring male convicts would demoralize the prison morale, the authorities transferred him to a cell in the women's ward. There the women inmates vied with one another in mending his garments and in showing him every possible kindness.

During his thirteen days in prison one of the best-known books, entitled *The Shooter at the Sun*, was released and he formulated and wrote on the pages of his memory another of his most popular novels, which later was published under the title of *Listening to the Voice in the Wall.*

He was confined in a solitary cell. Books and writing-paper were denied him. The following lines, written with a piece of charcoal on scraps of waste paper open tiny windows into his feelings and experience during those days:

"Midnight. The clock strikes one—two—. Wide awake I hound the prison vermin.

"Oh, the noise of a prison! It surpasses all expectation. How lively is the neighboring cell!

"Admirable indeed the thoughtfulness of the prison guard who planted the morning-glory and set it trailing its way upward to my iron-grated window.

"Sad is the sight—men, monkey-like, grasping the window ledge with both hands and lifting themselves up to get a peep out into the light.

"Back and forth, right and left, ceaselessly I pace my prison cell.

"How hard to bear—the sight of friends pressing their foreheads against the grated door of my cell and weeping bitterly.

"How grateful to one in prison is man's compassion as evidenced in a cup of cold water given.

"How I destest the dullness of this weary body as from time to time I give myself to meditation.

"Morning—evening—with many a shifting of my body, O God, I pour out my soul in strong crying unto Thee, Thou Rock of Ages!

"The sun that comes stealing in through the southward window does not withhold its shining.

"Alone in prison, but not without a friend—a fly-catching spider shares my solitude.

"There's one solace that never fails—the summer clouds which float in endless procession past the prison window.

"At times as I wring out the mop-rag and wipe up the prison floor I reflect upon my state and smile.

"Myself and God—only we two—how like the life of a monk in his cell.

"Confinement here three years, yea, even five, would be no hardship if God does not cast me off.

"The light is dim—there is no book. To closed eyes no light is necessary.

"Oh! the infinite beauty of the summer sun as it glistens and gleams on the granite of the prison wall.

"On a journey—round and round in my four-and-a-half-by-six solitary cell!

"I compose—on pieces of scrap paper, while walking round and round.

"The echo of the dock whistles and the pounding sledges penetrate even into this prison cell—how hateful is their sound!

"In the gathering dusk what a joy to hear the voices of the children echoing over the high prison wall.

"The prison vanishes while I listen, as in unison they sing, 'Guess who's your neighbor?'

"Pressing the mop to the window pane, I see on my faintly reflected face the big promise of a beard!

"The heat—all through the night, to and fro, to and fro, I wave the smuggled fan, creating a dream breeze.

"When times hangs heavy, water challenges to play; it soothes my face, cools my plunging arms, and provides a friendly frolic.

"My heart, immersed in twilight, is transformed at the time of prayer, to the likeness of the midday sky."

When the rumor spread that his release was near, 1,000 laborers quickly formed in line to march to the prison gate and welcome him. The pageantry of night spread over them as they set forth, each carrying a colored paper lantern and bearing the banners of a multitude of workers' guilds. The labor leaders, fearing that their presence might mean an extended detainment for their hero, pleaded with them to return to their homes. It was all in vain. They swore that they would camp before the gate until he was released.

After much good-natured discussion they finally yielded and withdrew to a near-by temple yard. There, on his release, they greeted their martyr leader with a fanfare of *banzai* (hurrahs) which shook Kobe's night. With songs and shouts they escorted him to his home in the slums. On reaching Shinkawa it was past midnight, but the whole district was astir. Men in their loin-cloths, women in their night clothing, children—just as God made them—to the last man, woman, and child they vied with one another in their eagerness to welcome him back. Strong men and women, whose eyes had long been tearless, were weeping, some in silence and others openly and unashamed.

The ex-prisoner celebrated his release by taking one hundred of the slum children for a day's frolic by the sea. For many of them it was their first train ride and their first outing. Some were sick; some cried for their mothers. All romped and played and ate to their hearts' content.

For one day Kagawa was neither slum reformer nor labor leader. He was simply a friend of little children. He played with them, ate with them, swam with them, and built castles in the sand similar to those he had made on the sand dunes of the Yoshino River at Awa.

Social and labor movements tend to be rough and turbulent, lacking in delicacy and eliminating the finer side of life. This labor leader, however, was first of all an idealist. He was an artist and a poet both in spirit and in temperament. He opposed class conflict, direct action, and violence. Even when the strike was at its height and the dock authorities and police tried to break the strikers' morale by resorting to brute force, he urged them to beat back the blow with love and not with hate and to put their reliance on the justice of their cause and in soul-force.

Yet his was no visionary leadership. He had a clearcut

program. He advocated the laborer's right to labor, freedom of domicile, an opportunity for mental development and to round out their personalities, freedom of marriage, freedom of migration, recreational privileges, liberty of speech, the right to organize, the right of associational contract and of religious freedom. He declared that the only basis of a true labor movement was to get past mechanistic and repetitive labor to labor that is creative, independent, and free.

He strove not only for the betterment of the laborer's lot, but of the laborer himself. Addressing them, he says: "The laborer must have no mean opinion of himself. Away with self-depreciation! Be conscious of your worth as a laborer and glory in your rôle.

"The producer's course is in creation. Don't get excited! A waste of nerve energy will get you nowhere. Be calm! Be steady! Let the imperialists and the capitalists do their worst. It matters not what the radicals and extremists say.

"There is but one course for the laborers. That is production motivated by love. The blind aping of imported ideas regarding labor unions, owners' unions, and the diversification of labor will never save the day. For Japanese laborers there is a Japanese way. That is invention and creation. Intelligently, accurately swing your hammer and watch the results. Unions are necessary, but labor problems can only be solved by the inner awakening of the laborer."

I ENJOY POVERTY. MANY POSSESSIONS ARE TO BE DEPLORED. IF one has nothing one's troubles are few. By this I do not mean that I want to lack the bare necessities of life. If in some way I can manage to live, a grand house is no attraction. Rather give me a hut among the trees. While the snail, the killifish, and the lotus leaf are my friends, I have no desire to be rich.

For this reason the labor movements with which I relate myself do not demand large possessions. They have but three demands—a chance to live, a chance to work, and a chance to show the marks of a man. I have no desire to participate in labor movements motivated by greed.

—KAGAWA'S *Meditations.*

V

THE LINE OF BATTLE LENGTHENS

MAN'S AFFINITY FOR THE SOIL

THIS CIVILIZATION OF STEEL AND CONCRETE SEPARATES MANkind from the soil. The soil is God's footstool. The scent of the soil heals me. I have no desire to become a civilized man. I want to live close to the soil.

—KAGAWA'S *Meditations*.

V

THE LINE OF BATTLE LENGTHENS

KAGAWA'S STUDY IN HIS SLUM LABORATORY LED HIM STILL farther afield. Historically the Japanese are an agrarian people. Japan's ancient civilization had its roots and came to flower in small country-conscious cities and in countless rural villages. During the feudal period the farmer ranked next to the Samurai in the social scale and in national importance. From the farm still springs much of the nation's moral fiber, its spirit of industry, and its sturdy manhood and womanhood.

The inauguration of a world commerce, the unfurling of the Japanese flag on all of the world's seas, and the rapid growth of industrialism gave a tremendous impetus to urban development. Yet fifty per cent of the people are still living on the land.

Japan is far famed for her natural beauty. The unique sublimity of her sacred Mount Fuji, the grandeur of her unbroken mountain ranges, the grace of her unending shore line, the beauty of the islands which stud her seas, the charm of her landlocked bays and the daintiness of her plum and cherry blossoms make her one of the world's garden spots. But Nature has been niggardly in her bestowal of natural resources.

The farmer's lot is peculiarly hard. Eighty-five per cent of the nation's area is mountainous. There are few expansive plains to convert into fields. As against Germany's cultivation of fifty per cent of her total territory, Japan's maximum possibility is eighteen per cent. Tragically small though it is, even this percentage can only be secured by terracing her mountainsides and bringing them under cultivation.

None of her land produces without fertilization. Forty-five per cent of her cultivated lands are irrigated rice-fields. Rice is the nation's main diet, but only a minor part of the world's population makes this its staple food. Thus, in time of shortage her farmers are in trouble. In case of a surplus there is no market.

In addition, over-population presents a serious problem. The whole of Japan proper could be tucked away in the State of California, leaving 10,000 square miles unoccupied. Yet close to 65,000,000 people are crowded into this limited space. Belgium has 300 people to the square kilometer; in Japan there are 1,000. Or if we take the cultivated area only, she has 2,722 people to the square mile. The landholdings are small, averaging one and a half acres for each farmer.

Even in the heyday of his power the Japanese farmer had a hand-to-hand fight with nature in his effort to sustain life. He was forever skirting the edge of poverty. The commercialization and industrialization of the nation's life and the resultant shift of the people's interest and energy to the cities brought him face to face with a major crisis.

The cost of living has soared, but the price of farm products has remained stationary, or slumped. Budgets can no longer be balanced. Farmers are going into bankruptcy at the rate of 10,000 a year. Annually 100,000 of the fittest and finest sons and daughters of the farms flock to the cities.

The tenant farmers, who compose forty-six per cent of the rural population, present an even darker picture. Under the prevailing tenant system they are compelled to turn over to capitalistic owners or to absentee landlords from fifty-five to seventy per cent of their crops. High land values and debts due the owners doom them, their children, and their children's children to the status of tenants all their days. Interest rates run from twenty to forty per cent. Sons inherit, not the family property, but the family debt. It resembles a system of serfdom. As a class they are poverty-stricken.

Kagawa discovered that then, as now, the slums were fed from this tenant peasant part of the population. The majority of the people around him hailed from the tenant farms. Worsted in their fight on the farm, they drifted to the cities and became the flotsam and jetsam which eventually landed in the slums.

He found that in spite of the good air, sunshine, and sanitary conditions of country life, impoverishment and the low standard of living of the peasant villages made the rate of infant mortality and the general death rate there higher than anywhere else in the Empire.

He traced the source of prostitution, both public and private, back to these villages. The owners of prostitute quarters and their procurers recruited their victims from this ignorant, destitute class. The factories and industrial plants, as well, combed these villages, and with the promise of better food and finer clothes lured multitudes of these peasant girls to the cities. There bitter disillusionment eventually drove many of them into a life of lust.

Disease, especially tuberculosis, ravaged these villages. The under-nourished condition of the peasants made them easy prey to disease and they furnished the largest per cent of the nation's 850,000 tubercular patients.

Undeterred by the heavy burdens he was already bearing and the enormity of the task, Kagawa determined to extend the battle line into the far-flung rural area and liberate the small farmers and the tenant peasants.

Simultaneous with the growth of self-consciousness and a sense of latent power among the laborers an awakening was sweeping over the tenant farmers. Disputes between them and the landowners—unheard of in old Japan—over the question of land rights and rental rates were increasing in frequency and in intensity. However, being unorganized and having to fight both the landowner and the police, the tenants inevitably suffered defeat.

In 1921 a group of peasants met in Kagawa's hut in Shinkawa and organized the first peasant union in Japan. Farmers' guilds had been in existence previous to this, but they were in the interest and under the control of the capitalistic farmers. Kagawa's house was made the headquarters of this new agrarian movement and branches were established all over the Empire. Assistance was given in cases of dispute with the landowners. A magazine was started, entitled *The Soil and Freedom.*

Later in the year an All Japan Peasants' Conference was held and the "Japan Peasants' Union" was publicly launched. Its organization caused a sensation. The fact that Kagawa and others who had participated in the Kawasaki and Mitsubishi strikes were elected officers caused much concern both to the landowners and to the government authorities.

The union's decision to take the part of the small landowners and of the tenants in their fight with the Landowners' Union at times of peasant uprisings greatly perplexed the capitalistic farmers and the absentee landlords. Its declared policy of promoting the enactment of a law to protect the tenants and to secure the repeal of the police regulation regarding the settlement of disputes between tenants and owners was considered radical. And its declared purpose of taking an active part in general elections in order to further the interests of the peasants, and its declaration in favor of the national ownership of the land, were looked upon as ultra radical.

The movement issued a manifesto in which it outlined its goal. "We purpose to nourish knowledge, improve our technique, cultivate our moral character, bring the element of enjoyment into life on the farm, and make the realization of a perfect rural civilization our goal.

"Standing for freedom of thought and assuming an attitude which will benefit society as a whole, we will love the truth. In order to realize an emancipation void of compromise, we will fight capitalism by organizing producers' guilds and attain the liberation of the poverty-suffering peasant."

It adopted as its program additional education for the rural peoples, the perfecting of rural industrial coöperatives, the organization of credit and other economic agencies, the betterment of rural housing and sanitary conditions, the encouragement of scientific agriculture, and the inauguration of a system of crop insurance.

Here again Kagawa rejected the red program of conflict and force. He advocated peaceful and parliamentary action and an evolutionary as against a revolutionary advance. He urged the peasants not to give themselves to the negative tactics of simply fighting for their rights, but to adopt such constructive measures as the introduction of new crops, the employment of new methods, and the setting up of mutual-aid coöperative agencies. Inasmuch as Japan has five times as much mountainous and three times as much forest area as she has level land, he suggested that more use be made of the mountains and that the forests be made productive in fruit and nuts.

He called their attention to the fact that capitalism has reached its present state through coöperative effort and called upon every village to organize itself scientifically like a city factory. He counseled them to pioneer in an effort to discover use for the nation's supposedly unusable land and in developing auxiliary work for their leisure winter-time.

He pointed out the need of a more scientific use of the soil, a more economic use of their time, a better division of labor, of increasing economic values through social cooperation and the use of machinery through the organization of coöperatives. On any and every occasion he declared that the most important thing of all was the remaking of the peasant himself.

The crusading urge has ever been strong in Kagawa; having adopted a cause, he flings himself into it with burning intensity. Trusting only in divine forces, he throws caution and soft words to the winds and sallies forth, as the knight-errants of old, to do battle for what he deems to be right.

As a patriot also this movement made a tremendous appeal to him. A disastrous reaction against farm life was sweeping over the youth of the rural area. Through the increased facilities for travel, the influence of the press, the coming and going of the young men conscripted for military service and through the stream of young people flocking to the cities for educational purposes, rural Japan was being brought into vital contact with modern city life.

The farmers were not sharing the benefits of the nation's modern material, cultural, and spiritual advance, and the contrast of the farmer's lot and life with that of his city brother had started a terrific drift from the farms to the cities.

Kagawa felt that there was no hope for the nation if its rural life went on the rocks. The city civilization is a consuming civilization, while that of the village is a producing one. Japan, unlike England, has no colonies to which she can look to make up a shortage in food supplies. Here in a critical sense it is true that her farmers must feed her.

He toured the Empire in the interests of the peasants' cause. He made them feel that a new hope had arisen on the horizon of their threatened domain. Everywhere he was acclaimed as their savior. Again, however, he ran pellmell into the opposition of intrenched interests and the police authorities. Both looked upon him as a dangerous agitator. The police did everything in their power to obstruct his work. In some places he was denied the right of assembly. Everywhere his speeches were severely censored. Detectives dogged his steps.

In one of his campaigns the police put him under surveillance and locked him up. When a police sergeant unlocked his cell door and informed him that the chief of police wished to see him, like Paul of old he replied, "if the chief wants to see me, let him come here." At that the representative of the law jerked him out of the cell and pulled him by force into the presence of the chief.

The chief's first words were: "I have read your books and greatly respect you. Tell me your impressions of your detention by the police." Kagawa, considering the question irrelevant and that the chief was trifling with his predicament, remained silent. When repeated attempts to get a reply were met with continued silence the chief flew into a rage and stormed at him, "You are insulting me!"

The prisoner, then looking his inquisitor right in the eye, quietly replied: "One so intelligent as you knows far more about police detention than I possibly can. Following the great earthquake, at the Cabinet's request, I served on the government's 'Imperial Economic Commission.' Here I have nothing to say. On my return to the capital I shall take up this matter directly with the authorities of the Department of Home Affairs and see if the Cabinet's attitude toward me has changed."

Hearing this, the color of the chief's face went through a series of kaleidoscopic changes as he shot out, "I thought you were a man, but I see that you belong to the rabble." The prisoner resumed a serene silence. In the face of bluster and bluff, silence and candor won the day. In a moment the strong arm of the law approached the silent figure standing before him and in subdued tones said: "Pardon my rudeness. You are at liberty." The disciple of non-resistance forgave and forgot.

However, Kagawa was no longer the unknown youth arrested in connection with the Kobe strike. His work in Shinkawa, the fame he had won in the literary world, and his leadership of the labor movement had made him a national figure. He had friends and followers by the thousands scattered through every walk of life. The police could harass him in his work, but they could not with impunity play fast and loose with his personal freedom.

When this episode came to the ears of the governor of the province he immediately summoned the police responsible for Kagawa's arrest and took steps to safeguard his own official head. It developed that Kagawa's only offense had been that in a tone of protest he had inquired of the police the reason for putting his fellow speakers under detention.

Under the drive of this ardent ally of the farming folk an agrarian movement was launched which promised to become nation-wide in its scope. It has assumed national proportions, but in the vicissitudes of time unlooked-for forces have emerged.

When one returns to the city fresh from the country a sympathy akin to pity goes out to the young women of gentle birth. These stupid creatures, whose existence is squeezed out of the peasants, the miners, and the factory workers, clothed in supple greenish garments, shod in soft footgear and leaning on the arm of a lover, they meander along the gaily lighted streets.

They seem wholly unconscious of the fact that the rouge on their cheeks was purchased at the cost of the peasants' blood. When one contemplates their manner of life so similar to that of a parasite, the impression deepens that the color of their skin resembles the color of an intestinal worm.

"No matter how elegant may be their beauty, it is after all a parasitic beauty. It is not the solemn beauty of the Grecian goddess, Athene, who took upon her lone shoulders the nation's anxieties and burdens. The beauty which I crave for the women of Japan is not a parasitic beauty, but the beauty of the goddess Athene.

"Nay, not only that, I yearn that the daughters of Japan shall have the beauty of Mary, the Holy Mother, who was able with a glad heart to offer up her own son to suffer for all mankind."

—Kagawa's *Meditations*.

VI

HEAD WINDS AND COUNTER CURRENTS

CHRIST'S FOOL

"CHRIST'S FOOL! A PUBLIC LAUGHINGSTOCK! TRULY THAT IS myself. Forty years, half of my allotted life, I have passed as Christ's fool. The world's so-called pleasures have all slipped by me. I have not leisurely witnessed even one cinematographic display. Tied up to society's rubbish-heap I have passed half my days.

As one narrow of mind and stubborn of will, a fit subject for ridicule, I have ticked off, in tears, day after day, half my life.

I have been summoned from the scenes of lust, caused to stand at the foot of the cross, and numbered among those who are labeled hypocrites, heathen, and anti-nationalists. But even in these circles I have not been sure of a welcome. Here, also, I have been ostracized as a heretic and a socialist, as one who is flippant and shallow.

But these things move me not. I am Christ's captive! A slave of the Cross! The world's fool! I am determined to abandon everything that bears the mark of this world, and, naked, sally forth along the road which leads upward to the state of the sanctified. If to others this seems foolish, there is no help for it."

—KAGAWA'S *Meditations*.

VI

HEAD WINDS AND COUNTER CURRENTS

THE EXPERIENCE IN SHINKAWA AND HIS EFFORTS TO EMANcipate the laborers and peasants convinced Kagawa that the existing social and economic order is radically wrong.

In Shinkawa, finding that the older people were wedded to their evil ways, his passion to save the children broke into a flame. These responded to the molding touch of his love-impelled personality. Gladly they exposed their plastic selves to his influence.

Eventually, however, they, too, were borne down by their surroundings. The boys went wrong. The girls were led astray. In spite of the power of his love for them an overpowering environment won out in the contest and enslaved them body and soul.

In the wider world of labor, and of the farm as well, the laborers and the peasants were no longer free men. They were bound down by an economic and social order which made them the slaves of circumstance and of economic determinism. He was forced to the conclusion that poverty and exploitation, wherever found, are two of man's chief foes, degrading, destroying monsters. They are wreckers of men. They play havoc with the finer human values and devastate society.

He, therefore, sallied forth on a sacred crusade to slay these demons. He became a warrior for the under-privileged and espoused the cause of the poor and of the propertyless, regardless of their class or connection.

He has been called an authority on social science. He

is rather a social seer, a creative pioneer in the field of social reconstruction. He is not satisfied with the speculative sciences. He is not a one-line specialist. His interests are too broad.

He might have made his mark in the world of science or of art. His mind is cast in the scientific mold. His thought processes are those of the scientist. But he does not have a one-track mind. His penetrating interest in life and his passionate love for men will not allow him to be a narrow, one-theme specialist.

Moreover, his mood is that of an artist. And like the Japanese artist, situations shape themselves in his mind and he pictures them with a few bold but simple strokes. He is a poet and has the poet's swift instinct for sensing the essentials of human situations. But here again his interest in folks will not permit him to be an out-of-touch-with-men artist.

He has to stand where the surge and flood of life runs strong and spend and be spent in the great laboratory and studio of the common man's workaday world.

He sees three twentieth-century tendencies which are tangling up the world's life. One of these is the concentration of populations in the cities, with a proportionate increase of physical, moral, and psychological dangers. He declares that full-orbed, high-toned personalities cannot be developed where people are robbed of the opportunity to fellowship with the friendly trees, smell the scent of the fresh grass, listen to the insects' chirp, hear the song of the wind, tarry by still waters with their healing quiet, bathe in the sunshine as it falls on valley and hill and mountainside and commune with nature in all her mystic moods.

He considers 40,000 the maximum population for an ideal city. Cities of over 200,000 he calls a calamity. In the abnormal life of such crowded centers civilization moves forward with shackled feet. Its face is set toward an untimely decay.

The second tendency is the concentration of machinery and the machine's mastery of men. This results in mere repetition and spells doom to creative labor. It mechanizes the laborer. It robs him of initiative, thwarts his creative instinct, destroys the urge to excel, stifles the passion to progress, and finally converts him into a machine or sends him forth to join the ever-increasing army of the unemployed.

The third tendency is the concentration of capital in the hands of the few, with its resultant increase of unfair distribution, exploitation, poverty, and economic determinism.

Kagawa is a social engineer, absorbed in actual programs rather than in academic speculations. His programs, however, are built on deep-going, strongly-buttressed principles. He believes in communism, but it is the communism of the early Christian Church and of Tolstoy, rather than of Karl Marx. As against the class hatred of Russian Communism he pleads for and passionately practices brotherly love. As against Marx's class conflict he advocates Tolstoy's non-resistance. In the building of a finer and fairer social order he believes in evolutionary rather than revolutionary processes.

He visualizes an order where men shall stand man to man, where human values shall be primary, and money and material things secondary. An order where the development of the individual shall be unhampered, where wealth shall be fairly distributed and a livelihood guaranteed to all.

He insists that social reconstruction must be brought about through change and organization rather than through violence and destruction. He reminds men that the French and Russian revolutions, both brought about through force, were accompanied by tragic economic, moral, and spiritual losses.

He is uncompromisingly opposed to a social and economic order in which some have a superabundance and others are in want. He emphasizes the fact that the heart and center of the change that must come is the abolition of the present predatory capitalistic system with its self-centered spirit, its profit motive, its exploitative methods, and its acquisitive goal.

He would socialize the community's and the world's wealth. He would build a social order where love shall be substituted for the present profit motive, where sympathetic coöperation shall replace the ruthless competition of the present, where service and sacrifice shall displace exploitation and selfish acquisition.

He believes that the avaricious passion to acquire and the profit-getting goal are the forces which are drying up the springs of understanding, consideration, and sympathy as between man and man and setting class against class, nation against nation, and race against race in a deadly economic and industrial war.

Only when capital is socialized and dominated by the spirit of mutual helpfulness, service, and sacrifice can real social reconstruction be realized. At the heart of it all there must be a readiness to understand, to forgive, and to love. The labor movement, the peasant's movement, any social movement, must first and foremost be moral and sacrificial; it must treat the rich and the poor alike.

Above all, in order to realize the necessary motive, spirit, and goal, social reconstruction must be centered in Christ. The spirit which led Christ to the cross must permeate it, vitalize it, and give it an abounding inner life. The human heart must be resculptured. Man-made morality has created the present avaricious economic system and degenerate politics. Christ alone can make all things new. In other words, the labor movement, the peasant movement, any and every social movement must be a movement toward brotherhood. The spirit of Christ, the carpenter, must be the soul and creative dynamic of all real social reconstruction.

Recognizing that there must be a transition period he exhorts Christian capitalists to cut their mode of living down to the minimum standard of the average man, to devote their capital to lifting the whole level of social life, to make every effort to socialize their own and the world's capital and turn it from the present capitalistic acquisitive basis into coöperative channels. He urges him to renounce the acquisitive motive and use his capital and energy to convert capital, wherever found, to a coöperative service basis.

He admonishes the Christian laborer to purify his motives, desires, and life, to discriminate against no one, rich or poor, and to love all men with sincerity. To support his union, but not with selfish or aggressive motives, and to lead it toward altruistic as against materialistic goals. He must not be so absorbed in his group as to forget society as a whole. His consciousness and interest must transcend his class and take in the welfare of his fellows of whatever name or connection.

The laborer must recognize the transitory period through which the world is at present passing and acknowledge that there are capitalists who are sincerely seeking for light and ready to do what is right. If his employer be of this type he should coöperate with him in any attempt to socialize capital through evolutionary rather than revolutionary methods.

If his employer be an exploiter he should strive to show

him the error of his ways, but not by resorting to violent measures. If his employer is endeavoring to inaugurate a new social order he should coöperate with him to the utmost. He should, however, never lose sight of the final goal—the socialization of capital.

The drive of a new and challenging social program carried Kagawa's movement far afield in its early stages. The conservatives and stand-patters, both in politics and in religion, held aloof or aggressively fought his advance, but his admirers and followers were legion. Among high and low those who yearned for a more just social system acclaimed him as their hero and peerless leader.

Then came the invasion of the radical lefts with their materialistic interpretation of the universe and of life, their non-idealistic and anti-religious program and their appeal to class strife and force. This propaganda marched with seven-league boots through the ranks of the laborers and peasants, dividing them into rights and lefts, with the lefts an aggressive and growing majority. When Kagawa refused to see red, refused to resort to force, and refused to set class against class, there developed a revolt against his leadership both among the laborers and among the peasants. They faded out of the picture in alarming numbers and left him a leader of a minority movement.

Hitherto opposition to him and his work had come from exploiting employers, avaricious landowners, official quarters, and static religionists. Now the guns were turned on him from his own camp. He was again the lonely prophet crying out against materialism, capitalism, the clash of the classes, violence, and static religion. He was as lonely as his Lord when He failed to fulfill the material, political, and transient aspirations of the people of His day.

In his magazine he wrote: "Just now everyone speaks

evil of me. Every magazine counts it a virtue to attack me. I am the target of the red socialists, the anarchists, the capitalists, of foul-mouthed literary men, of pro-government newspaper men, of Buddhists who do not know me, and of Christians of the obstinate bigoted type.

"Enemies come at me from every direction. Here among the poor I am beaten until I bleed. Now for two weeks I have been disabled and unable to perform any form of work. Yet through these attacks I will be well polished! I am not conscious of having done wrong. I am scoffed at as a pacifist and as an apostle of love. There is nothing to do but bear it.

"In the presence of truth, persecution and oppression are powerless. In the presence of truth, steel chains and prison bars melt away. Friends, fear not the truth! Taste deeply of the truth as it is in Jesus and advance!"

On the heels of the ultra-radical lefts' invasion came Russian communism with its high-pressure propaganda. It ran an even deeper wedge into Kagawa's following and threatened utterly to eclipse him.

His passion to build a new order, however, feeds upon opposition, pain, and sacrifice. Undaunted, he grappled with this new foe. He came out as the fiery exponent of a social democracy based on parliamentary rule, universal suffrage, respect for the right of the minority, and freedom for all. He attacked the proletarian dictatorship, the direct action, the suppression of the minority, and the force employed by the Russian communists. He declared that this was a "denial of democracy and a fettering of freedom."

These declarations made Kagawa, who had been the idol of the laboring classes, the target for their criticism and the object of their bitter hatred. They branded him a traitor to their cause and an ally of bourgeois democracy with its inherent despotism.

The red wing of the labor movement in Kobe—the very center of his selfless activities—issued a proclamation to the laborers of the nation:

"Bury him! Bury Kagawa, the hypocrite, who is unceasingly striving to make dupes of us, of the propertyless class. This false humanitarian taking advantage of us, hides behind the beautiful name of religion and scatters a deadening anæsthetic among us. Here in Kobe he appears in the form of a savior, but his message has no relation whatever to the life of the propertyless class.

"Is he not trying to save us from our desperate condition by getting us resigned to our fate through belief in a traditional religion which is steeped in falsehood and deception?

"No matter how long and loud we shout 'amen' our empty stomachs are not filled. Where is the gate to his heaven of amens where real salvation is to be found? Kagawa himself, in the midst of all his dreamy silly talk and twaddle, does not know.

"While we are being misled by his religion the capitalists are quietly sleeping in their downy beds.

"To the eyes of a true warrior standing on the propertyless men's battle line, Kagawa is a hateful enemy. Remove his mask! Tear off his steel-like hide! Banish him from our midst!"

The Japan Peasants' Union, whose organizing genius he had been, was also disrupted by the red propaganda. From the peasants another scathing manifesto was trumpeted across the land:

"Kagawa is a pleader for the favored classes. Ostracize him! We young men of the propertyless class have no desire to come under the influence of his anæsthetic.

"He throws our movement into confusion. We are summoned to expose before the masses this backer of a class-divided social order. It is our duty to bury this disturber of the propertyless class's movement. He must not be allowed to throw our battle line into disorder."

Kagawa, like all men of strong conviction, uncompromising statement, and clear-cut program, is today one of the most passionately loved and desperately hated men in the Empire. The profit-motivated, exploiting capitalist, the revolutionary communist, the anti-religion socialist, the reactionary politician, and the religious leader who worships the god of "things-as-they-are" see in him a mischief-maker and a menace.

Declaring that the purpose of a social movement is not to destroy society, but to rebuild it, he presses the battle for the building of a new social and economic order. Believing that society will leap forward toward the realization of this ideal if everyone is sympathetically coöperating instead of ruthlessly competing, he pours his life into the organization among all groups and classes, of coöperatives, producers' and consumers' guilds, mutual-help guilds, sick-aid societies, and credit associations.

In order to enable the under-privileged to find life an enlarging, ever-growing experience and an opportunity to develop their personalities he organizes short-term laborers' and peasants' schools with courses adapted to their special needs.

He is the head of the Osaka Spinners' Union, the adviser of the reorganized All-Japan Peasant Union, and the leader of the laborers and peasants who have not fallen for the red program. He helps them to organize and rushes to their aid in times of conflict with exploiting employers.

Everywhere and all the time he pleads for an evolutionary socialization of capital so that every man may, directly or indirectly, have his fair share, and as a result of honest creative toil be assured of a simple livelihood.

Kagawa's opponents say that his star has begun to set. In certain circles he undoubtedly has lost prestige. The radicals among the laborers, the reds among the peasants, and the Marxian-minded everywhere repudiate him and his program. The students who see red no longer acclaim him as their prophet.

For weal or for woe, as far as Kagawa is concerned, officialdom and the Christian Church have shifted their stand so far toward his point of view that he appears today to the reds and the radicals as a tool of both and a traitor to the liberal cause.

The bitter opposition which he faced from the police and from official quarters, during the early years of his work, has spent its force. Not only so, but by a strange turn of events he is today often embarrassed by the government's patronage. Repeatedly in his speaking campaigns in the provinces the central authorities at Tokyo send advance notice to the heads of public educational institutions instructing them to give him a hearing and to urge their students to attend his meetings, even though they are of an out-and-out Christian character. This puts him in the anomalous position of appearing to be a government propagandist in his war on the materialistic, anti-religious program of the reds and their advocacy of force and revolution.

It is a long, long way from the present chaos to the new social order as this seer sees it, but he leaps along the level stretches and eagerly climbs the steep ascents, borne on by a mystical call to do big things in hastening its coming.

His star is still in the high heavens, leading him on to new and ever more daring adventures.

IN THIS WORLD THERE IS NOTHING SO ABSURD AS OWNERSHIP. To the child a bead is more to be desired than a diamond. To the miser a gold coin seems of more value than inventive genius. In a word, proprietorship reflects the purpose which moves men in any age.

Thus for those who make production their purpose in life, ownership is beside the mark. To the inventor neither the bead nor the gold coin necessarily has any value.

Ownership is like a shell. The only one who profits by it is he who shuts himself up within it. To him who desires to reach upward and grow, it is only a hindrance. As the shell exists only for the spineless animals, so those who cling to the right of ownership may be called mollusca.

In an age of invention and discovery it is but natural that there should be a great upheaval in the thinking regarding this question of ownership so strenuously advocated by the spineless species. The mollusca have my sympathy.

—KAGAWA'S *Meditations.*

VII

GIVING A LEAD TO LEADERS

KAGAWA HAS RENDERED TROJAN SERVICE NOT ONLY TO THE poor and the under-privileged, but he has brought the impact of his many-sided personality to bear upon men and problems in high places.

His leap into Shinkawa put the slums on the map of the national consciousness. His sacrificial sharing of the life of these submerged peoples for fourteen years and eight months lifted them into the spotlight, where all saw the sordidness and sadness of their lot and sensed the hopelessness of their cry. More than that, it put them on the nation's conscience.

With words that were heart's blood made vocal, and with a pen that flamed, he showed that they were not so much the victims of their own as of society's sins. Unsparingly he laid the guilt upon the corporate life of the whole nation.

He toured the Empire and from the platform pleaded their cause. He bombarded the press with articles graphically picturing concrete cases and giving the results of his first-hand study. His prolific pen worked feverishly putting book after book, dealing with various phases of the problem of the slums, into the hands of the nation's large reading public.

For months—yes, years—his was a lone voice in the wilderness. He beat himself against an immovable wall of inherent inertia. The slums had always existed and always would. Fate decrees that the fittest shall survive and the beaten sink to the bottom. Let them remain there. Why all this fuss about a lot of alley spawn?

This modern knight-errant opens his heart and home to all kinds and conditions of men, but to defeat he bolts the door. Even though it smashes its way into his presence, it is left standing unrecognized. The nation's indifference only fanned the flame which was burning in his heart.

Unceasingly he made the awakening of the nation's conscience the goal of his unwearied activity. His book, entitled *The Psychology of the Poor*, was a scholarly study of the causes of poverty as related to the problem of the slums and suggestions as to its cure.

At length, under his incessant attacks, a break appeared in the solid wall of inertia and indifference. Publicists and thoughtful people began to insist that the slum was not an institution fixed by fate. Men and women with a social consciousness and religious leaders here and there began to say that the slum must go. Slowly the public conscience began to wake and wince.

In 1926 the government, moved by Kagawa's words and writings, set itself to wiping out the slums in the Empire's largest six cities—Tokyo, Osaka, Yokohama, Kobe, Kyoto and Nagoya—in a period of six years, and appropriated $10,000,000 for this purpose. This is one of the most daring and far-seeing pieces of modern social legislation.

The six-by-six cell homes of Shinkawa are no more. The foul, disease-breeding, criminal-producing slums in Japan's six major cities are no more. The cell-like homes have been destroyed and modern municipal apartment houses have been erected in their stead. The narrow filthy alleys have given place to streets, paved and properly sewered. The way has been cleared for the sunshine, the light, and the air to do their healing and redeeming work.

Would that it could also be recorded that the poor

masses who milled through those slums are no more. Regarding this Kagawa says, "Better housing conditions alone are not enough. This must be followed by other social legislation. There must be a minimum wage, sick aid, unemployment insurance, old-age pensions, and mothers' pensions before poverty can be wiped out."

The problem of poverty has not as yet been solved. Some of the inhabitants of these slums are showing a tendency to colonize in other outlying districts. But the slum in Japan is on the run. It will take eternal vigilance and progressive adventurous social legislation to complete what has been so well begun. Yet to have demonstrated to the world that the slum, the festering sore of great cities in every land, can be eliminated is an accomplishment of maximum import.

The great earthquake of 1923 laid waste two-thirds of the Empire's capital, a city, including the suburbs, of 5,000,000 people. It also laid low the entire city of Yokohama, the nation's most prosperous port. One hundred thousand lives were lost and property destroyed to the value of five and a half billions of dollars.

Tokyo is the official and political center and the educational Mecca of the nation. Industrially and commercially Osaka is forging to the front, but even this progressive city waits for Tokyo to give the sign. To a unique degree the entire nation takes the cue from the capital. Every new movement in any field starts from this center. As goes Tokyo so goes the nation.

The earthquake thrust a knock-out blow right into this beating heart of the Empire. Not only were 100,000 lives snuffed out and an incalculable amount of property destroyed, but the railways and street cars, the telegraph and telephone, the postal service, communications of every kind, were put out of commission. The radio and air service were then still in their infancy.

The fire finished the devastation which the earthquake began. The result was that no building, no machine, no material, not even tools, remained in the whole stricken area with which to begin operations anew.

It was a time that called for the best brains and keenest minds the Empire possessed. The Cabinet feeling that it could not cope with the situation alone set up an Imperial Economic Commission to assist the government in the titanic work of reconstruction.

One hundred and eighty of the nation's ablest men in official life were invited to serve on this commission. The Premier himself acted as its chairman. By a dizzy turn of events Toyohiko Kagawa, whom a few years before the police authorities had hounded and treated as a dangerous demagogue, was made a member of this important body. He alone was chosen from the ranks. The others were all government officials of high position.

He agreed to serve. However, in order to forestall the impression that he had surrendered to the authorities with whom he so often found himself in conflict, he issued a public statement declaring that because of the national crisis he had called a truce for a period of one year and would coöperate to the utmost with the government and its appointed agents. His work on this commission was epoch-making. The plan that was finally adopted and carried out bore in no uncertain characters the marks of his workmanship.

While serving on this commission he put through an Anti-Exploitation Land Act. This law provides that where the wealthy hold land purely for speculative purposes the nation shall have the right to confiscate and turn it to productive ends.

He knew labor and the laborer as no other man, and in quick succession he was drafted for service on the government's Commission on Unemployment, its Commission on Labor Exchanges, and its Commission on Emigration.

It is his policy to coöperate with the government when by so doing he can serve the people, but never simply to help the party in power. He laughingly remarks that when he helps the government the officials greet him with a smile, but when he turns to assist his first and undying love, the proletariat, detectives begin to darken his trail.

Kagawa's incessant efforts in behalf of labor led the way to the removal of the police ban on labor organizations. In 1925 the law against trade unionism was amended granting Japanese laborers the long-fought-for legal right to organize.

To him also must be given large credit for the organization of Japan's Labor Party. Because of its division into militant left, center, and right wings this party has had a hectic career. Nevertheless, it has served as a rallying center for the proletarians of the Empire. It has given them a voice in national affairs. It has elected proletarians to membership in the Imperial Parliament. It has made the proletarian movement a force to be reckoned with in the economic and political life of the nation.

Repeatedly Kagawa has been urged to run for Parliament on the Labor Party's ticket. He has persistently refused. He works in season and out of season to bring harmony and unity into the party. He gives to its funds until he bleeds. He throws himself without stint into campaigns for proletarians running for Parliament. He himself, however, refuses a seat among the mighty, lest this should build a barrier between him and the poor and the under-privileged to whose cause he has dedicated his life.

The winter of 1930-31 was one of the darkest which the city of Tokyo has experienced. The whole nation was in the throes of a financial slump. The bottom had dropped out of business and industry. The capital was staggering under an enormous debt incurred through its post-earthquake reconstruction program.

Unemployment was growing by leaps and bounds. The poor were in a pitiful plight. By the thousands both the unemployed and the very poor were sleeping out in the open, beaten by the winter winds and drenched by the chilling rain or the driving snow.

Mayor Horikiri was no perfunctory official. He was a human being, deeply concerned about the suffering of the people whose welfare had been thrust into his hands. The city was spending $5,000,000 a year on its program of social relief. Its Social Welfare Bureau had a staff of over eight hundred, but it was not grappling with the situation. The mayor wanted a man who would put the Bureau on an efficient basis, enable it to come to grips with the crisis, and put on an effective program of relief.

According to long accepted practice the mayor was not at liberty to go outside of official circles in selecting a chief for his Welfare Bureau. Worse still, it already had a head, a hold over from a former regime.

Disregarding precedent, the mayor turned to Kagawa, urged him to become Head of the city's Social Welfare Bureau and help him and the city to cut their way through the crisis. The salary would be $9,000 a year and an automobile for his own use.

The mayor's action caused a sensation. It raised a row in the City Council—because of the appointee's views on political and social questions. The conservatives and reactionaries attacked him because of his socialistic views. The socialists and radicals attacked him because of his religious idealism. Within the Bureau itself he was called an idealist, an impractical dreamer, and intrigue against him was rife.

Kagawa at the time was engaged in a nation-wide evangelistic crusade. He could not see his way to accept the headship of the Bureau. He, however, never turns a deaf ear to a call of distress, and, acceding to the mayor's second proposition, became the Bureau's chief adviser.

The mayor's offer of a salary of $9,000 he absolutely refused. With this money he could have supported for an entire year the three social settlements which he personally conducts in Kobe, Osaka, and Tokyo. These institutions desperately needed those funds. They are constantly facing a financial famine. But he never chooses the easy way. Tokyo was in distress. He would not add one iota to the city's burdens. He would serve only on the condition that there be no salary. He insisted on rendering a service with the sting of sacrifice in it.

The mayor asked for the resignation of the head of the Bureau and left the post vacant in order to give Kagawa a free hand. The new chief adviser was thus virtually head of the department. For more than a year he spent ten days of each month reorganizing the Bureau and ministering to the needs of the city's sufferers.

He appeared at his office in the stately City Hall in the $1.85 laborer's suit which he wore in the slums. His first official act was to visit, in person, the centers of poverty and distress. He secured shelter for those exposed to the cold of winter. He fed the hungry. He preached to the masses.

Tokyo has a modern system of street railways and transportation, but the bulk of its food supplies is still distributed by means of 11,000 house-boats which ply on 218 miles of canals running like arteries into every section of the city. Thirty-one thousand people are employed on these boats, half of whom live in the boats' six-by-nine-foot holds. Often a family of twelve is crowded into the boathold.

He found the living conditions among these boatmen to be unspeakably bad. Being constantly on the move, they had no medical advantages, no school privileges for the children—in this city of schools—and no social advantages for old or young. He provided visiting nurses, established dormitories for the children of school age, and places for the parents to sleep.

He started eleven new social settlements in as many sections where the need was the greatest. He made provisions to assist the poor in giving a decent burial to their dead.

In five months after assuming office he prepared and put through the City Council a scheme of unemployment insurance by which the city's civic unemployed are registered at the Municipal Employment Bureaus and guaranteed work or given a grant every third day during the period of their enforced unemployment. It also provides that available labor under the city shall be equally distributed among these registered unemployed.

To Kagawa belongs thus the credit not only of initiating the movement for wiping out the slums in six cities of the Empire, but in inducing its chief city to take the second step in solving the problem of poverty by adopting a scheme which guarantees its own workers employment or gives them protection while unemployed. In the field of social legislation this is a pioneer step not only in Japan, but throughout the Orient.

At times the lead he gives to leaders has the ring and the sting of the prophet's severity. In 1927 the three major religions of Japan—Shinto, Buddhism, and Christianity—summoned a National Religious Conference for the purpose of emphasizing the fundamental truths which they hold in common and pressing them home to the hearts and consciences of the people.

The conference had the support of the key leaders of the three faiths and was attended by 2,000 delegates representing every section of the Empire. Shinto priests in rich robes set off with gold brocade, Buddhist priests in ornate vestments, Christian pastors in formal black apparel, gave the gathering the aspect of a parliament of religions or a colorful pageant of the nation's faiths.

It was Kagawa's hour on the program. He appeared in his plain workingman's garb. With words that flashed and flamed he pictured the condition of the laborers, the factory workers, the peasants, the fishing-folk, the miners, and the very poor.

"Their stomachs are empty. They have no place to lay their heads. For these who have neither food nor shelter what help is there in mere preaching? God desires mercy, not ritual.

"The time has come when the priests of the shrines and temples and the pastors of churches should come out of their somnolence and face realities.

"You Buddhists! Read again your scriptures and find in them the spirit which animated your pioneers. If you cannot rediscover and reincarnate their spirit, roll up your scrolls and carry them back to India whence they came.

"You Shintoists! If you cannot grasp the vision which

impels to service for the weakest and the most unfortunate, of what avail are your numerous and elaborate rituals?

"And you Christians! Shame on you for erecting huge and costly churches and failing to follow the Man born in a manger and buried in another's tomb."

He warned them against the evil influence of exploiting capitalism and charged them of consciously or unconsciously being its tools.

His fiery words threw the stately conclave into an uproar. Ringing protests were made from the floor. The executive committee hurriedly met. A plenary session of the conference was called and the disturbing prophet expelled. This done, the delegates settled down to their regular routine as though they had done their duty by God and man.

The reactions outside of the conference were various. Some praised. Others blamed. One Christian editor wrote, "I regret the arrogant attitude and words of Kagawa. Did he think that that was the time and place to set himself up in God's place and as a prophet belabor the worldly and wicked religious leaders?

"Doubtless from his point of view they are lukewarm. They do not rush from the church and monastery and bury themselves as he does among the poor and the laborers. But society is not simple. It cannot be revolutionized in one fell swoop. People's tastes and tempers differ.

"Why cannot he be more human and more sympathetic with religious leaders in their present difficult situation? Why cannot he have real consideration for their distress and declare, 'though our arenas differ, let us work together in remaking society and in burying the capitalistic civilization'?"

Nevertheless, this daring utterance made a profound impression. It was made front-page news in all of the leading dailies and focused the nation's attention upon the conference and its work. Instead of denouncing the speaker and depriving him of his status as a delegate the conference should by all rights have passed a resolution of thanks to him for saving it from innocuous insignificance and making it a real force for advanced religious thinking and for social righteousness. But prophets are never praised.

Kagawa's pen is one of the most prolific and versatile among modern writers. There is no village in the Empire, no matter how remote or how isolated, into which his books have not penetrated. To wide-awake, forward-looking village leaders these books point the way to a new day both for themselves and for their village.

Moreover, men of high estate, through his writings, make excursions into his mind, his spirit, and his manner of life. The late Premier Hamaguchi, soon after his installation into the highest office the nation can bestow, announced to the pressmen that he had spent his week-end reading *Across the Death Line.*

Although still on the sunny side of forty-five, he has published fifty books, of which 1,200,000 copies have been sold. He is also the author of thirty pamphlets and thirty-five leaflets. Three hundred thousand of the former, and 5,000,000 of the latter have gone out bearing his message across the Empire. At the present time he has ten more books in various stages of preparation.

His books take him into the diverse fields of religion, philosophy, poetry, biology, pedagogy, economics, politics, and labor. His pamphlets and leaflets are campaign documents in the fight against evil, irreligion, social injustice, and vice.

His pen always has a purpose. His fiction is problem novels dealing with religion, politics, poverty, and social purity. They are human documents teeming with real life. All have made "best seller" records. *Across the Death Line* reached the high watermark of 250,000 copies; *The Shooter at the Sun*, 110,000; *Passing from Star to Star*, 100,000, and *A Grain of Wheat*, just recently off the press, has already reached the 100,000 record-making figure.

One reason his fiction captures the imagination of the reading public and leaps to the place of first sellers is that back of it is the challenging personality of the author, his life in the slums, and his leadership of great social and religious movements. The author and his activity constantly furnish front-page news in the daily press.

In sending out a book containing a collection of his lectures he says: "Many read my books. But I am a soldier of movements to awaken the conscience and he who hears the outcry of my conscience is my true friend. To bury 550 brothels, stop the flow of $750,000,000 worth of liquor, accomplish the salvation of 100,000 poor, hasten the day of the emancipation of 9,430,000 laborers toiling in various fields and liberate 20,000,000 tenant farmers—may this day come speedily—this is my highest hope as I send out this book to the reading world.

"The human conscience itself is politics, economics, education, science, and therefore the education of the conscience is of first importance. If the conscience is educated, politics, economics, education, and science will take care of themselves. These addresses are the outcries of conscience itself."

For twenty-five years this knight-errant has stood in the fierce light which beats upon one who plays the rôle of prophet, crusader, and leader, but it has not spoiled his simple, childlike soul, lessened his love for the poor, or dampened his ardor to serve the under-privileged.

IT WAS A RELIGIOUS CONCLAVE WHICH KILLED CHRIST. IT WAS the Brahman elders who laughed Buddha to scorn. Those who thwart and destroy movements which spring from a conscience newly awakened are always the hangers-on of authority and of moneyed might. They are the so-called maintainers of order. They manufacture justice to suit their own advantage and coerce the people in the name of God. And of all concerned, God Himself surely is the most embarrassed.

Jesus looked beyond the Jewish nation. To Buddha the ruin of the Kubera Palace was not the crucial problem. Truth revolts against hypocrisy. If this be true, Christ was slain on the cross as a son of revolt. Socrates was handed the cup of hemlock on the ground that he was an anti-nationalist.

Those who fail to take man's conscience into account and attempt to bind the truth by authority alone are on the path which leads most speedily to the nation's ruin. Spain's decline began with the religious Inquisition. Before enacting religious regulations make known first of all the God whose abode is in the conscience.

Truth must not fear a revolt against hypocrisy. It is hypocrisy not truth which destroys the nation. Out of the chaos caused by truth there always springs a new order for coming generations.

—KAGAWA'S *Meditations.*

VIII

A FIGHTING PACIFIST

THE FUTILITY OF FORCE

THERE ARE THOSE WHO ARGUE THAT BRUTE FORCE WILL SOLVE all problems. If force is such an important factor it would be well always to employ earthquakes and volcanic eruptions. They ought to make a far greater contribution to the evolution of human society than Newton or Edison. The evolution of the social order is not governed by militarists, militaristic dictators, or anarchists who rely on force.

Social evolution is impelled upward by means of selection, ideals, exertion, invention, and motives which produce the highest good. A world built by force will be destroyed by force. Ask me not to live in so precarious a world. I place no hope whatever in force, no matter what form it takes.

Nothing lifts us upward except the power which comes from within—science, invention, discovery, art, drama, morals, religion, and exertion directed toward the supremest good. If these forces which issue forth from within are omitted, outward forces are powerless. My reliance is on the unseen, inner forces.

—KAGAWA'S *Meditations*.

VIII

A FIGHTING PACIFIST

KAGAWA'S PARADOXICAL PERSONALITY MAKES HIM AT THE same time an ardent pacifist and one of the keenest of fighters. Personally he is a conscientious, consistent non-resister. In Shinkawa he persistently refused to turn to the police for protection against the threats and attacks of drunken bullies and desperate dagger-bearing ruffians. Without any show of resistance he quietly listened to their blustering, bloodthirsty harangue as a friend listens to a tale told by a bosom friend. Usually the result was that their violent urge to fight suddenly sprung a leak and they slunk away.

When they came maddened with liquor and lusting for blood he adopted a different technique. "When bullies grabbed me by the collar, prepared to beat me black and blue, I quietly looked them right in the eye and without any sense of fear, resentment, or anger prayed to God for their forgiveness. Under that cool, calm gaze they soon broke, and muttering: 'It isn't worth the trouble. What's to be gained in killing such a fellow?' walked away. Again and again this has been my experience."

But at times he paid dearly for his pacifist principles. "He was a murderer and none of the fourteen doss-houses in the district would give him shelter. He promised to reform, but a friend of his evil days set him off on a spree. He bought drink, charging it to my account. I had to pay the bill. For a time I thought it better to allow him six dollars a month than to have him fighting and murdering.

"Then he intrigued with other ruffians to attack me, and

at a critical stage in their onslaught dramatically appeared and drove them away. For this he demanded a stipend as my protector. When I saw through the game and refused, he beat me up, knocked out my teeth, and disfigured my face."

Kagawa saw much of his work in liberating labor and the peasants, into which he had poured the richest and reddest blood of his life, drift out of his reach because he refused to resort to violence. Yet he was unmoved.

"Man cannot be saved through opposition and violence. Violence cannot be rationalized. Economic movements and social reconstruction are a growth.

"It is only when force is eliminated that economic movements realize their highest goal. Economics based on force belong not to the realm of scholarship, but of soldiership. The only true road is through love and the wisdom which wells up from within.

"For this reason all the communistic experiments of history that failed to make love central went on the rocks. Love alone is the way out. Love alone can create a just social order. Let me rely on love and on love only.

"Emancipation which is based on force is not true emancipation. Out of such social reconstruction there springs up a new exploiting class with an unsound system of thought. In order to cover up their self-centeredness and dullness of heart they create a new philosophy and in turn despoil others."

Believing that individuals and social movements should rely only on soul force and the power of love, he is absolutely opposed to war and all that relates to it.

His was the only Japanese name which appeared on the manifesto against military conscription presented to the League of Nations, which bore the signatures of Tagore,

Gandhi, Einstein, Romaine Rolland, and other eminent leaders in the war on war. This put him at the top of the black list among the ultra-nationalists and the militarists of his own nation.

In 1928 he organized the National Anti-War League of Japan. This organization embraces not only the right wing of the laborers and the propertyless class, but progressives in the regular political parties, scholars, religious leaders, and literary lights.

This League adopted a platform with three planks:

1. We are opposed to war and all preparations for war.
2. We are opposed to all aggressive imperialistic political, economic, and uplift movements.
3. We are opposed to the advocacy of aggression, to imperialistic utterances, and to the oppression of weaker groups and peoples.

Its program covers a far-flung range of activities:

1. A nation-wide agitation against war.
2. Carrying the Paris Peace Pact into effect.
3. The establishment of the International Court of Justice as a permanent and fully empowered tribunal.
4. Putting on an educational program in behalf of anti-war ideals.
5. Advocating the rescinding of Article One in the constitution of the League of Nations.
6. Unifying all the peace and anti-war organizations in the Empire.
7. Bringing about a solidarity between the anti-war organizations of the world.
8. Agitating for a decrease of expenditure for military purposes.
9. Opposition to the trade in munitions.
10. Opposition to education for imperialistic ends.

This move brought down upon him the wrath of the reactionaries and the ultra-nationalists. From the platform and in the press they accused him of being the tool of American pacifists and of Russian communists.

They denounced him as a traitor to his country. Such a furore was created that his life was threatened and the police put him under detention in order to protect him. He also came under the suspicions of the powers that be and they took steps to soft-pedal him and those who joined this League.

Kagawa is, however, no negative, white-livered pacifist. His pacificism is of the militant type. He has a keen taste for moral and spiritual warfare. He is a fiery idealist. He has been called "The Agitating Poet."

In Shinkawa quarrels were as common as briers on the brier bush. It was the quarrel center of Kobe. In a circle of a hundred houses around Kagawa's hut there averaged a quarrel a day. He was often called in as referee, a dangerous undertaking. It was the custom for the arbiter to cut off his little finger and hand it to the participants as a pledge of impartiality. Many an arbitrator lost not only his finger, but his life. Regardless of the difficulty or the danger, Kagawa gladly gave himself to the work of peace-making.

The effect these quarrels had upon him reveals a militant strain deeply imbedded in his make-up. "One reason I entered the slum is my fondness for fights. Not because they often end in murder, but because of the whole-souledness which characterizes the contestants. Not because of the foul words which fly and the abuse which is exchanged, but because justice is struggling for victory. Not because the swords flash, but because blood is being freely offered up. When the red blood flows, man recovers Adam's original undisguised soul. I wanted to see that naked soul.

"When the swords flash through the air and the red-hot charcoal braziers fly through space, when the red blood flows and the corpse lies prone in the narrow alley, I give myself to quiet thought and prayer. Man's soberest and sincerest moment is when he sees life freely given.

"Among the numerous things of interest about man, the most fascinating of all is where the flesh and the spirit are at swords' points. When one visualizes on the ethereal screen their fighting figures and hears their exchange of blows."

Kagawa has discovered the moral equivalent of war. He makes frontal attacks on disease, drinking, smoking, and sexual vice because he yearns "that the young shall be morally and physically virile and valiant." He is one of the most active leaders in the Association for the Abolition of Leprosy and in the Society for the Eradication of Tuberculosis.

Out of the furnace of his experience in the slums he considers liquor one of the nation's deadliest foes. In Shinkawa he was surrounded by drink-enslaved men. They squatted themselves in front of him and breathed their liquor-laden breaths into his face by the hour. They wept their eyes out in his presence in order to win his sympathy. They preached to him for unlimited periods. Some sat in utter silence hour after hour. Others rough-housed and made his hut seem like the aftermath of battle. But he never rebuked these drunken men. He felt that they were not responsible for their actions. He waited until they came to themselves and then exhausted every resource in an effort to redeem them.

"From the economic point of view liquor is one of the

greatest causes of poverty. This nation consumes $750,000,000 of liquor a year. It spends $100,200,000 annually for tobacco, twice the amount spent on education. What hope is there of saving the poor in the face of these foes? Poverty is the normal result of such a state of affairs. Japan lost in the Japanese-Russian war 55,000 men during a period of two years, but every year 170,000 of our people die from brain disease caused by the use of alcohol."

Early and late he stands on the firing-line, hurling shell after shell into the ranks of the brothel-keepers and their henchmen. "After almost fifteen years of life in the slums I have discovered that two things are responsible for all the sin and shame which reign there—liquor and syphilis.

"If they do not attack these people directly they come upon them with calamitous effects through heredity. Eighty to ninety per cent of the criminals as well are the matured harvest of alcohol and sexual sin."

The exploiters of the underworld recognize in this knight-errant a valiant foe. A paper published in their interest pictures him in lurid colors.

"Burn him! Burn Kagawa! A traitor who stirred up the Kawasaki dock laborers to strike. A socialist who endangers the nation's future. A hypocrite who prates about God's love. For a purpose he lives in the slums and wears a laborer's suit.

"Men of intelligence recognize that this hypocrite should be ostracized from society. His attack on our national system of public prostitution, advocating the methods of 'strike' and 'boycott' on the part of the inmates and patrons, shows him up as a dangerous character. The strike and boycott are both contrary to law and he who advocates their use should be dealt with as a lawbreaker.

"He is a dreaded revolutionist. He stirs up quiet diligent laborers, inciting them to strike. He is a sore in the side not only of the capitalist but, of the whole nation. He strives to overthrow the present social order.

"How many are the faithful laborers who have been led astray by him! How many the earnest capitalists who have had their enterprise trampled upon by him! How many are the young who have been ruined for life by him!

"Still he is not satisfied. He attempts to turn the good and faithful prostitutes against their masters and would introduce the strike even into the sacred precincts of the houses of prostitution. In so doing he would push up his name on the flag of fame.

"In his attack on the legitimate business of prostitution, his advocacy of socialism and his efforts to overthrow the present economic order he is a traitor to the nation."

Such defiance on the part of the enemy only results in this champion of purity tightening his belt and throwing himself with greater determination into the fight.

"Temperance workers and social evil reformers today are too refined and timid. Those who are engaged in social reform and attempt to remake society must expect opposition and rough handling."

Here is a man who fights on real battle fronts and whose weapons are not of steel. He fights with ideas packed with dynamite and ideals that blaze the path to a new world. His weapons are of the spirit and probe to the depths, taking hold of hell itself.

Determinative though the influence of environment is, he never forgets that God-centered spiritual forces are mightier. "Many today are putting so much emphasis on the influence of environment that they destroy the freedom of the will. To bring the unseen motive into God's presence and harmonize the hidden purpose with God's will is the only way of creating true righteousness."

This fighting pacifist, with ideas and ideals, love and soul force, as his weapons, is winning out in his warfare. The government has recently taken steps to wipe out leprosy by establishing a series of isolation hospitals. The nation is coming to grips with the tuberculosis scourge. The temperance movement is gathering momentum. Fifty-three villages have already adopted prohibition. Two million people have joined temperance organizations.

The upholders of the nation's present system of public prostitution are fighting with their backs to the wall. Seven prefectures have outlawed brothels, and campaigns are on in the remaining thirty-seven to secure legislation which will wipe them out of existence.

No one would say that the credit for these initial victories belongs to Kagawa alone. Many others have heroically held their sector of the battle front. But this militant pacifist has been and is one of the hardest and heaviest hitters.

Many things are set in motion through rebellious action and the spirit of dispute. As for me, however, I cannot conceive of this being life at its best. The life that moves me most is the life that so abounds in love that it forgives even its enemies. When I see a bourgeois whose attitude is wrong but who concedes that he is at fault and offers an understanding heart, or when I behold the great love of a proletarian who makes amends for the failures of the bourgeois as though they were his own, I cannot refrain from tears.

Some one will doubtless ask, "Is such a foolish thing possible?" Yet One there was with as great a soul as this who trod this earth of ours. His name was called "Wonderful." He was called Jesus. A son of a carpenter and a carpenter himself. I have found the highway which I must walk in His atoning life. Love is mightier than rebellion.

—KAGAWA'S *Meditations*.

IX

A CRUSADE AND ITS CRUSADER

THE EFFICACY OF EVANGELISM

SOME SAY THAT IT IS PURE PRESUMPTION TO URGE REPENTANCE upon people and proclaim a gospel of salvation. They insist that only he who is out of step with the times indulges in such arrogant conduct. Among those who argue in this fashion, the wayward, the egoist, the willful and those who press for their own selfish way abound.

Others, again, contend that it is wrong to urge repentance upon one's fellows and attempt to save them, because such action issues from a sense of superiority.

Were it possible for men to live an isolated, sundered life, repentance and salvation might not be necessary. In that case the individual might be left to settle his own affairs. But where the syphilitic disease of a debauchee poisons his descendants even to the fourth generation, and where the alcohol which men drink smites with a curse even to the tenth generation, one cannot but implore people to repent.

Even more imperative is the necessity of urging repentance upon moneyed men who, because of their unawakened state, tyrannize over tens of thousands of toilers and treat them as wage-slaves.

From the individualistic standpoint there may be no need to press for repentance and preach salvation, but where life takes on a social aspect these two moral activities become imperative.

For the individualist in whose consciousness society is still unborn, a world where self-gratification is the norm may seem right, but society will never come to its own on that basis.

Because the building of a moral social order known as the Kingdom of God was explicit and inherent in the teachings of Jesus, His religion and the way of the present-day proponents of individualism naturally clash. He who calls evangelism antiquated is a novice as regards life. When the destiny of mankind as a whole is considered, we must acknowledge that Christ made no mistake in his passionate effort to save.

—KAGAWA's *Meditations.*

IX

A CRUSADE AND ITS CRUSADER

THE CHRISTIAN IN KAGAWA OVERSHADOWS THE SOCIALIST. The follower of the Nazarene in him takes precedence over the advocate of economic reform. The prophet in his soul is Christian, capitalized and written in letters of light. Of all the emotions which race through his finely strung personality, the passion to make Christ known and to adventurously incarnate his life is uppermost and controlling. He is a flaming apostle of the Kingdom.

The most luminous and long-to-be-remembered hours during his nearly fifteen years in Shinkawa were those when, in his six-by-six hut or out on the open street he strove to stem the downward drift of the lives around him by crying out: "God is love! God is love!" and proclaiming Christ as the redeeming expression of that love.

His richest and most rewarding experience as a labor leader was getting up at four o'clock in the morning, going down to the docks and wharves in Kobe, and preaching to the laborers and freight-handlers as they gathered for their day's work.

The singing of "Jesus, Keep Me Near the Cross"—his favorite hymn—gathered the men around him. The colored Japanese lantern which he carried threw a dim light upon their upturned faces as they stood there in the retreating darkness of the early dawn.

There are times when the emotions race through his entire being, causing the tears to fall like a sudden summer shower. These sons of toil, exploited, sinning and sinned against, stirred his deepest emotions, and with the tears streaming down his cheeks he told them of the Carpenter of Nazareth, the son of the producers' God—a God who from the beginning of time and even now never ceases to toil.

Some felt strangely moved by his words, others by his tears. To still others it was a strange tale, and even while he was preaching they squatted on the ground beside him and began to gamble in the flickering light of his lantern. But whether they listened or tossed the dice, his love brooded over them like the love of a mother over her first-born.

Kagawa is a religious genius, but he is human. He knows human nature, human weaknesses, human needs, human sorrow, human aspirations, and is always more than anything else concerned with folks.

In his messages he uses the language of the people. He speaks in terms of their daily needs and deals with the problems which try their souls. The woof of his religion is present, pressing, problem-burdened life; its web is life unseen, endless, and centered in God.

Such distinctions as secular and religious are unknown to him. Life is not divided into compartments, with Christianity functioning only in one isolated section. When he thinks of life, or any phase of life, he spontaneously applies the teaching and example of Christ to any and every phase of it. When Christ's teachings are the subject of his thoughts he instinctively thinks in terms of life and every expression of it.

Kagawa's Christ has lost none of his interest in the common life of the common man. He has lost none of his sympathy for the masses. He has lost none of his appreciation of personality, even though it be poor, outcast, and neglected. He has lost none of his sense of injustice as regards the rich and the poor. He has lost none of his spirit of adventure in endeavoring to bring in a finer and fairer order.

Furthermore, Kagawa's Christ has lost none of his spirit of sacrifice, his readiness to stake everything in an effort to lift life—every life and all of life—to the place where it shall become large and full and an alluring quest for mystic realities.

In these days when many religious leaders have ceased to be prophets pointing the way to a better day, here is a crusader adventurously blazing a pioneers' trail toward a Christian social order. Kagawa has a passion not only to preach Christ, but to practice Him. He indulges in no side-stepping, no trimming, no toning down, no explaining away of the high and hard things which Jesus taught and did.

His Gospel is not an emasculated, soft-souled Gospel. The Cross is central in it. It is not, however, a theological or a theoretical Cross. Nor is it simply a Cross of long ago. It is a Cross which alone can solve every present-day problem and set right every tangled situation. It is a Cross which takes the face and form of every brother-man who is not getting a fair, full chance and presses with paralyzing weight on this crusaders' heart. It is a Cross which alone can furnish the dynamic that will lift this weary, wayward world back to God.

Kagawa is not a traditionalist. He is essentially a pioneer. He blazes new trails. He is out for a Christian-social as well as a Christian-world order. But he gladly "stands on the proffered shoulders of the past" as he faces the challenge of the future. He takes the historical approach to every question.

His study of the Huguenot movement and its influence on the people of France convinced him that the power of the Christian Church to fashion the moral, social, industrial, and political ideals of a nation is determined by the momentum of its impact. This aroused a conviction that until the Christians of Japan number one million strong they cannot become a creative force mighty enough to fashion the nation's life according to the Christian pattern.

As he pondered over this he heard a mystical call to initiate a nation-moving evangelistic crusade which should systematically work its way into every section of the Empire, reach out into every class, and group and carry on until the Christian constituency in this land shall number a round million.

Like every dynamic idea, this one staggered men of lesser mold. Few had faith to believe that Japanese Christianity, which after seventy years of heroic endeavor only numbers 300,000 followers—including the Greek and Roman Catholic Communions—could through a crusade such as he proposed, no matter how continuous or how far-reaching its scope, push the number up to so full a figure.

The clearness and urgency of the call, however, grew in Kagawa's heart. Undaunted, he went forward with the project. Unceasingly he kept the idea before the minds of his friends and followers. Continuously he moved an ever-increasing number of individuals and groups to catch the vision and vitalize it with creative faith and prevailing prayer.

Backed by this crusader's personality and ardent spirit, the vision illumined the hearts and fired the imaginations of an increasing number until the project assumed the proportions of a movement.

In 1929 Kagawa sounded a clarion call to all who had caught the vision to unite in inaugurating the crusade. Gradually it gathered momentum. A year later a Central Committee, representative of the whole Christian movement, was set up to organize and direct the venture, and under the title of "The Kingdom of God Movement" it was definitely launched with simultaneous campaigns in the six largest cities of the Empire.

This movement was conceived in one of Kagawa's mystical moods. Under God he brought it to birth. It became evident, however, that even so flaming a personality as his could not move the nation single-handed. The rank and file both of the pastors and of the church members had to be mobilized. The prayer-power and soul-power of the church had to be enlisted and concentrated on this crusade in order that the tides of the Spirit might be released and God be given a chance to break out anew upon the nation's life.

Kagawa is still the throbbing heart of the movement. He is still the spiritual genius and dynamic personality around which it centers. It has, however, expanded from a Kagawa campaign to one embracing the organized Christian forces of the nation. It has flowered into an All Christians' Crusade.

From every conceivable human angle this crusade is undertaking the impossible. It is attempting to rally every Christian and every church behind a united nation-wide movement and create a spiritual solidarity among the Christian forces of the Japanese Empire. This is something new under the sun, not only in this but in any land.

It is engaged in an effort to evangelize every group and class, 30,000,000 farmers; 5,278,000 industrial and factory workers; 1,500,000 fishing-folk; 459,000 miners; 1,033,000 employees in transportation services, and the 1,158,000 toilers engaged on public works—classes which the Japanese Christian Church and the various foreign missions affiliated with it have left practically untouched during the seventy years of Christian history in this land.

The winning of the students in the nation's secondary, technical, and higher schools—2,500,000 strong—the leaders of tomorrow and the makers of future Japan, is another of the movement's major objectives.

It has, moreover, set out to humanize and Christianize the social and industrial order through making Jesus' way of life the norm in every relationship, in the relation of the ruler and the ruled, the capitalist and the laborer, the employer and the employee, the owner and the tenant, wherever man meets man. This has never been seriously attempted in any land. Indeed, a large section of the older church of the West never has and does not now recognize this as an integral part of its legitimate program.

The Gospel of Christ, according to Kagawa and his fellow crusaders, brings full-rounded emancipation, economic, political, physical, psychological, and social both for the individual and for society. Only as Christ's way of life and the cross-principle become operative in the whole realm of life will the Master's prayer, "Thy kingdom come. Thy will be done in earth as it is in heaven," be realized.

Kagawa declares, "If we do not discount the Gospel, but take it seriously and live it adventurously, we will be able to do far more than Russian communism ever dreams of doing in building a better world."

This is not a one-line preaching campaign. But the verbal proclamation of the Gospel looms large in its program. For the three-year period of this movement Kagawa has committed his social settlement and slum reclamation work in the three cities of Tokyo, Osaka, and Kobe to trusted co-workers and is giving himself wholly to this crusade to Christianize Japan.

In the mass evangelism program of the movement he is the central figure, though ably assisted by more than two-score of pastors, evangelists, laymen, laywomen, and missionaries endowed with gifts enabling them effectively to address the masses in large gatherings.

This crusader is a master of assemblies. His half-blind eyes enable him to see only in dim outline the people in the immediate vicinity of the platform. When he faces an audience he has the feeling of "looking into a heavy, blinding mist." But his great sensitive soul, with a mysterious psychic power, unerringly reads the mind and the mood of his hearers.

His addresses are characterized by quiet fervor and moving power. He sways the multitudes who everywhere gather to hear him. Himself a man of action, his addresses lead men to action. Throughout his messages there are the delicate touches of a poet and the telling action and gestures of an actor.

However, the most vivid and abiding impression left with the listeners is that of a mind alert, a soul on fire, an overwhelming passion in possession of a disease-riddled body all dedicated to one high, unselfish purpose and working together in absolute harmony toward its realization.

Since the inception of this crusade he has, under the planning of the movement's Central Committee, gone systematically from city to city and from town to town, speaking everywhere to capacity houses. During that time 25,000 people have met his challenge to break with the past and venture with Christ into a new way of life.

It is his purpose and the Committee's plan that he shall participate in campaigns in every city, every town, and in many rural sections so that when the campaign comes to a close he shall have practically covered the Empire.

In order to fuse the Christian forces of the nation into a compact unit and enable them to move forward into this crusade as an articulate whole, ninety Regional Committees have been organized. These take the initiative in setting up campaigns for their respective areas. The Central Committee renders them every help possible in their local campaigns. They in turn share their accumulative experience with the larger movement.

An almost one-hundred-per-cent attendance of her children in the public primary schools—the exact figure being ninety-nine and seven-tenths per cent—gives Japan the world's record for literacy. Her people are inveterate readers. As a means of entering this open door, *The Kingdom of God Weekly* was launched as the organ of the movement. It has become an evangelizing medium of tremendous power, penetrating into homes and hearts where the spoken word cannot go. The movement is also sowing the country with Christian literature in pamphlet and booklet form. Kagawa and other leaders have prepared, especially for this campaign, a series of booklets setting forth various aspects of the Christian message. These are being eagerly bought and read.

Recognizing that no one evangel nor any group of evangels can realize the high goal toward which this crusade is moving, an effort is being made to raise up an army of 5,000 lay preachers—men and women who in the course of their daily round shall give earnest witness to the faith that is in them. To attain this objective, Training Institutes for Christians are being held in every city and center for the purpose of mobilizing the laity and training them for effective participation in the movement.

Another outstanding objective of this campaign is the evangelization of the 12,000 unreached rural villages. The drive into this vast virgin field is being centered around short-term Peasant Gospel Schools. These schools bring together fifteen or twenty picked young people from the villages of certain areas and, during a period of a week or ten days each year, give them intensive training for Christian and community leadership in their respective localities. Many of these young people return to their homes and start something—a Sunday school, or a Bible class, or a study group or a recreational center or some other form of community helpfulness. Through their creative example and effort they remake the entire atmosphere and life of their village.

The program of the campaign provides for special evangelistic efforts for every unreached group and class. Efforts are being made to take the Gospel to the factories, to the fishing-hamlets, to the mines—wherever men toil and women weep.

In the labor and industrial field preparations have been made to hold conferences of Christians who employ laborers in large numbers as well as Christian factory owners, to study such fundamental questions as capitalism, labor conditions, hours, wages, and the relation of employers and employees, with a view to finding a solution for these problems in harmony with the teachings and spirit of Christ.

As an integral part of this campaign, Kagawa is pleading for a revival of the brotherhood movement and communal life which characterized the Christian Church in her fresh fervent youth when her life of love made the pagan world marvel. He contends that the church has become institutionalized, devotes herself to theorizing and formal teaching, while the times call for a Gospel incarnated in love-intoxicated personalities and demonstrated in institutions which sacrifice and serve. By a return to the communal life through the establishment of sick aid funds and the organization of mutual help societies, the church must concretely demonstrate what Christian ideals actually mean and what a Christian community really is.

The scandal of the modern church is that, although she has the unemployed, the under-privileged and the poor right among her own membership, too often she does not lift a hand to help them. The unjust inequalities which characterize society as a whole exist within the church as well, and go unrebuked and unameliorated. It is this situation that leaves the laborer, the unemployed, and men and women with a keen sense of social justice cold when the church is mentioned.

In order to remove this scandal, Kagawa would have every church a genuine working brotherhood where those who have share with those who are in want. A place where sharing, service, and sacrifice are not mere shibboleths, but creative forces hastening the coming of the Kingdom for which Christ so passionately prayed.

This crusader repudiates a diluted, colorless Christianity, but he believes that the church has a divine mandate to permeate society, with Christian ideas and ideals. He urges it, therefore, to strive to bring about an evolutionary change from the present competitive, capitalistic economic order to one of service and helpfulness, by the organization of co-operatives in every community.

The Kingdom of God Movement which Kagawa visualizes is not confined to the present three-year effort. To him this is only the preliminary stage of a far larger, ever-unfolding movement.

"The Kingdom of God is an eternal aspiration after God and for a program that unfolds forever. It is ever moving upward and onward toward a perfectly organized and unselfish society.

"The goal of the Kingdom of God Movement is a Christian society, the Christianization of every community. It envisages an economic social order where love shall be the dominant motive and the principle of the Cross spontaneously practiced.

"In this new order the life of the community will be organized on a coöperative, as against a cut-throat, competitive basis, through producers', consumers', and credit coöperatives. Service will replace acquisition by means of sick benefits, mothers' pensions, unemployment insurance, old age pensions, and other forms of communal helpfulness and social economic coöperation.

"The Gospel of Christ is for society as well as for the individual. Unless Christ is made the center of the social movement, the world is doomed. If Christians were living the program which Christ laid down in the Sermon on the Mount, there would be no place for the reds and Russian communism in the world today.

"Neither communism nor socialism will ever bring in the Golden Age. Their goals are too near and too clear. Christ was wise when he declared, 'My Kingdom is not of this world.' The Kingdom of God is eternally evolving. No member of the Kingdom can ever be satisfied. Beyond any stage of realization its ideals will flame up ahead.

"We must, therefore, continually do our uttermost for every phase of life, physical, psychological, moral, economic, and social. They all belong to the Kingdom enterprise. The physical, psychological, and moral belong to the individual, and the social and economic to the social phase of the Kingdom.

"The Kingdom of God starts here, but evolves forever. We are given the formula for its realization, but, like the sons of God, 'it hath not yet appeared' what its consummation shall be.

"The formula is the Golden Rule plus the blood of Christ. The blood of Christ is circulating all the time and everywhere. It goes into every festering place, every weak

place, every place of need. It goes with healing, restoring, and upbuilding power into every phase of life, both for the individual and for society.

"Moreover, the coöperative movement must be worldwide in its scope. It must leap across national boundaries in its outlook. This is Gandhi's mistake. He thinks too much in terms of India. The coöperative movement which will bring in the Kingdom of God must be international in scope and aim.

"Concretely, it must get rid of tariffs and tariff walls. Freedom of trade on an international basis must be realized, or small nations like Denmark, Norway, Holland, Poland, Switzerland, Siam, and Japan will be crushed out of existence.

"Above all, this international coöperative movement must be Christianized. The League of Nations and the International Court of Justice must be given power to deal with economic questions and these institutions must be reinforced and vitalized with an inner, Christian life. It is the church's mission to create for them a Christian atmosphere and permeate them with the spirit of Christ.

"This larger vision of the Kingdom of God, instead of minimizing the need of the oral proclamation of the Gospel, raises that need to the *n*th degree. An ever-increasing emphasis must be placed upon evangelism as one of the God-given means of realizing this Christian social and world order.

"However, this evangelism also must be international in its method and scope. The distinction of sending and receiving countries must be done away with. The old traditional missions whose major goal is the building of denominations must pass out of the picture. The whole world Christian enterprise must be put on a coöperative and sharing basis."

This crusader was born and reared in a land where for centuries the deep-toned Buddhist bells have sounded a mystic call to his fathers to join in the quest for God. Today he, in turn, rings deep-toned bells summoning the Christians of every land to venture with Christ along the high, hard way which will build the Kingdom of God among men.

BY DIVINE REVELATION IS MEANT THE ENTRANCE OF TRUTH into the depth of living. As long as the truth does not hold sway over the whole life, cognition and life are two separate entities, God and man are living apart from each other. When the truth penetrates into the whole warp and woof of life, then for the first time God becomes man's motive power and the guiding spirit of all his ways.

Therefore, he who seeks for the divine revelation will not find God through the theory of cognition. First of all let him endeavor to create values. Let him liberate those who are oppressed, feed those who are in want, give sight to the blind, find a way to enrich the poor. Then will he be able to see divine revelations every day.

This is the truth. The emancipators see God daily. God whispers to them. They stand in His presence. While the religionists of the study are seeking for divine revelation through cognition the God of life reveals Himself in the midst of life itself. The divine revelation is not closed. False scholars and false religious teachers are setting it at naught.

—KAGAWA'S *Meditations.*

X

A MODERN MYSTIC

THE IMMEDIACY OF GOD

THE LIFE OF EVERY MOMENT IS A PHENOMENON OF GOD'S heart. Every task is the combustion of the flame of God. He greets us in the kitchen. He gazes intently upon us at the well-curb. In the bustle and hustle of the factory or when hanging on the strap in the crowded car, we breathe God. When we lift the iron sledge and are hammering out the steel, we are in God's bosom.

This is the mood of the true soul. To be drunk, not with liquor, but with God. To feast to one's heart's content, not on food, but on God. In dreaming and in waking hours, in sorrow and in laughter, to walk in a world flooded with light, this is a phenomenon experienced only by those who truly know the soul's art.

—KAGAWA'S *Meditations.*

X

A MODERN MYSTIC

KAGAWA TAKES HIS PLACE WITH THE MYSTIC SOULS IN every age who have been strangely sensitive to the wooings and ways of the Eternal and whose insight into the unseen has enabled them to hold high a torch for a world ever dull and slow to understand the things of the spirit.

From his earliest Christian experience he leaped right into the midstream of the mystic's conception and experience of God. Through the years he has steeped his soul in the writings and mystical experiences of the masters among these men and women of the inner light. In Saint Francis, Charles Wesley, George Fox, Madame Guyon, and others of that charmed circle he has found congenial spirits and has taken his way through the world in intimate fellowship with them.

He has, however, been no mere imitator. In this sceptical, cynical, materialistic age he moves through life to the music of the unseen and duplicates in his own soul the experience of those of old who walked and talked with God face to face.

All of the epoch-making visions and decisions of his epoch-making life date back to hours when his soul drew aside the curtain which separates the seen from the unseen and held high converse with God.

His header into the slums, his espousal of the laborers' cause, his decision to emancipate the peasant poor and his call to inaugurate the Kingdom of God Movement, all came at times when his soul experienced an occult clarity as the result of a season of fasting, meditation, and long-continued prayer.

Such mystical moods and experiences stand like heaven-touching milestones all along the pathway of his life. Times when he not only quietly pondered and penetrated far into an uncharted land, but grappled and wrestled with his soul until, with a clear eye and an understanding heart, he saw the unseen and heard the unheard.

He has hours of ecstatic contemplation when he loses himself in God and allows Him to play full and free upon every key of his personality.

"Heaven's rain of mercy, and joy which wells up from my soul's depths, this is my portion. As I sit quietly meditating, with my eyes fixed intently before me, an ecstasy of exquisite bliss floods in upon me and I partake of the ever-flowing fountain of God's nectar. The wall, the straw mats, the charcoal-container by my side, even this body of mine, afflicted with many a thorn, all become the tender palm of God's caressing hand.

"Held tightly in the tender palm of His hand, God's red arteries warm my benumbed soul. God's love is stronger than the love of a lover. His light is my food. His purity is the air which I breathe. Even though I behold not His face, the tip of His index finger is ever imaged in my eye. And though the scribbling of the nail tip of God's forefinger be counted a commonplace, yet it is more beautiful than the sky at dawn.

"I did not behold the creation of the universe but to me, held spellbound in the caress of God's palm, there comes an understanding of the fact that everything which happens within the spheres is an everflowing fountain of ecstasy for me and mankind."

There is nothing nebulous or intangible about his experience of God. To him God is infinitely more than "The

Absolute," more than "Cosmic Energy," and more than "Elan Vital." He is not "marginal and vague, but focal and dynamic." He is the Father, the Comrade, the Comforter, the great Ally—all that the human heart in all ages has yearned and experienced Him to be. His immediacy is supremely real.

"The wisdom of Christ consists in his refusal to theorize. He who delights in theorizing would better steer clear of Jesus. Religion is not a theory. It is life. Jesus found God without the use of theories. His was a Godlike God.

"The God of the philosophers—the Infinite, the Absolute, the Omniscient, the Omnipotent, the Omnipresent, the Immanent Reality—he did not see God in such terms as these. His God was inherently too much of a Father, he was inherently too much of a Shepherd, to be recognized in such ideology.

"To the gentle Jesus the gentle God revealed Himself. To the men of this age who can only understand through theories, only a theoretical God will be revealed. I abstain from theories and in simplicity of soul call the great heart of the universe "Father." He who loves theories may call it law, or energy if he will. Let me be numbered among the gentle-minded."

This radiant Comrade not only breaks in upon his luminous hours, but walks with him along all the busy, bustling ways of life. "In Jesus' way lies the secret of maintaining a heart of religious devotion even while linked to this vulgar world and surrounded by those absorbed with the things of time. When the hands are immersed in the washtub, when fanning the coals under the oven with the bamboo blower, when writing figures, over and over, at the accountant's desk, when exposed to the sun, buried in the mud of the paddy-field, when standing before the smelting furnace ablaze with 1,600 degrees of heat—unless even at such times as these we live the same religious life as when at prayer in the monastery the world will never be saved.

"Even though a man transports his body to the mountains, if he leaves his heart in the village there is no hope for his salvation. Furthermore, a religion so weak that it is unable to save the village even though it succeeds in saving those who can escape to the mountains cannot save the whole man.

"Mountain retreats and religious systems can never constitute a Gospel. True salvation begins with the heart. If salvation is not realized in the crowd and in the bustling city, a true, living religion has not yet begun its work."

The place of this mystic is not in the monastery, but in the arena. He is no ecstatic dreamer sailing among the stars. He is no rhapsodist, lost in rapture. He has the prophet's fiery soul which resents and rebukes wrong wherever he finds it. He has the reformer's crusading spirit which sets out to right these wrongs.

"There are theologians, preachers, and religious leaders, not a few, who think that the essential thing about Christianity is to clothe Christ with forms and formulas. They look with disdain upon those who actually follow Christ and toil and moil motivated by brotherly love and a passion to serve.

"To them formulating definitions about the truth is a higher thing and of more value than to emancipate the under-privileged masses. They conceive pulpit religion to be much more refined than movements for the actual realization of brotherly love among men. Hence, religion becomes calloused and an empty cast-off shell. The religion which Jesus taught was diametrically the opposite of this.

He set up no definitions about God, but taught the actual practical practice of love."

This mystic has a modern mind. He looks upon every problem from the modern point of view. He accepts the findings of modern science and glories in them. He approaches every question from the scientific as well as the mystic angle.

In order to understand man he delves into biology. To fit himself as an efficient social engineer he studies psychology and sociology with all their modern implications. With a passion to build a more just social order he majors in economics with all their present-day ramifications and probes deep into the hidden workings of modern finance.

His methodology is modern. Insisting that every power which modern man possesses is given of God, he lays hold of every discovery and advance that has been made and utilizes them as Heaven provided means with which to build a God-centered and God-ruled social and world order.

"I am opposed to setting bounds for the mysterious and seeking for truth only through the senses. For me, reason, laws, and mechanical discoveries all belong to the realm of mystery. I believe that nothing has done so much to lay bare the world of mystery as modern science.

"The reason science lost the sense of mystery is because it severed relations with life. If once it is discovered that there is life at the heart of science and that mechanics, laws, and reason are all the handmaidens of life, then it will be clear that these mechanical discoveries, laws, and reason are but windows opening into the world of mystery.

"I am a scientific mystic. The more scientific I am the more I feel that I am penetrating deeply into God's world. Especially in the domain of biology do I feel as though

I am talking with God face to face. The world which is not cut off from life does not need Kant's agnosticism. Through life I discover a purpose even in a mechanical world. Science is the mystery of mysteries. It is the divine revelation of revelations."

The saints of old—Saint Francis of Assisi, Saint Theresa of Avila, Saint Anthony of Padua, Saint Catherine of Siena—hied themselves away to some spot of historic interest and natural beauty where the surroundings and nature at its best engendered beautiful thoughts and noble deeds.

The Saint of Shinkawa, on the contrary, plunges into life at its lowest and worst. With compelling earnestness he lays hold on the unseen forces and builds for eternity, but his passion and purpose is to bring God's Kingdom down out of the clouds and realize it here among the meanest and neediest of men. His mysticism is not narrowly individualistic but broadly social. It is not emotional, but ethical.

"Oh, my soul! My soul! Do you hear God's pain-pitched cry as He suffers because of the world's sore distress? "Yes, I hear it! I hear it! I feel within me the beating pulse of the universe. I hear the deep sighings of God.

"God gives growth to all things. He brings back those who go astray. He is the mighty will which exerts itself to the uttermost to redeem those who have wandered far from the fold. A keen sense of this presses in upon my inner being. The strong sighs of God resound like earth rumblings across my soul.

"When sight was fully mine this did not enter my consciousness, but, as the day of darkness lengthens, echoes which then I failed to recognize now sound and resound through my entire being. In a word, I am forced to feel that, having so largely lost my eyesight, the power to see has extended into every part and parcel of my person.

"Of this I am acutely conscious. The might of God's creative and regenerative power pours through my entire being like inrushing electric waves. God is indeed life itself. Hid in Him I grow."

The mysticism of this modern mystic is deeply rooted in meditation and prayer. In the early morning, invariably at four o'clock for a full hour—far removed from the distractions of the life around him, he opens his total personality to God and to spiritual influences.

"If in the rush of home cares or of our daily toil, in the early morning or late at night we take time for reflection and heart preparation for the coming day or review the one which is gone and in stillness spend time in prayer to God, those will become the most joyous moments of our days.

"In order to hear the voice of the voiceless God we must be quiet, silent before Him. In man's daily life this is of all things the most important. If we listen, God will speak to us in a language all His own.

"It is said that Gandhi, of India, has his devotions at four in the morning and then rests again until early dawn. There is naturally a difference in the religious discipline of the tropics and the religious experience of the Temperate Zone. We would do well, however, to copy India in our religious life.

"To observe religious worship in the early morning is man's wisest way. The midnight hour also brings profound revelations, yet there is a danger of illusions, resulting from nervous debility, if one meditates until midnight following the weariness of the day.

"After reposeful sleep, prayer in the early dawn, fellowshiping with the morning star, brings to human beings the supremest of blessings. Jesus also loved the hours before the dawn. Many of the followers of the Zen sect of Buddhism have this practice. Forever let me be a child of the early dawn."

This lively consciousness that every moment and in every move he is venturing with God has produced a serenity and a poise that baffle the uninitiated. Notwithstanding his many-sided activity and constantly crowded program, there is no sense of stress or strain in his presence. He goes from one to another of the manifold tasks and responsibilities that press upon him as unhurried and tranquil as though the eternal years were his.

"If one lives for a long time immersed in God's grace there stretches across one's inner soul a calm which nothing can destroy. When, guarded by five officers of the law, I was thrown into prison pending trial, when marching with a mob of 15,000 people along a street seething with riot, when threatened with daggers in the hands of desperadoes, the jewel of peace, hidden away in my soul, was in no wise disturbed. When in an automobile crash the city tram rumbled on over me, that inner peace was still maintained. Even when a chronic eye disease threatened to rob me of my sight I experienced no swells on the calm sea of my soul.

"Polished like a mirror, this calm reflects in itself every passing circumstance of life, but its occurrence leaves no turbidity on the surface. Criticism, abuse, ridicule, slander, all these simply serve as polishing powder in the process of further burnishing the mirror-like calm in my heart.

"Even I myself stand amazed at this calm! This tranquillity within is so composed and sustained that it borders on the absurd. Neither the earth's quaking nor the alarm of fire nor blizzard nor avalanche can shake it. I have seen too much that is abominable and witnessed too much of sorrow. The result is that even cruelty cannot ruffle this calm.

"One thing and one thing only can break up this tranquillity of soul. That is deep emotion issuing from love-stirred tears. This calm, which neither wickedness nor danger can disturb, is mightily moved when I behold pure love attempting to redeem the world. Then the fountain of my soul starts to ripple under a drenching shower of tears like the untimely waves which rise when a squall falls upon the surface of the sea."

This mystic insight into the things of the unseen not only removes the veil between him and his Maker, but makes him akin with Nature. She speaks to him in a language which he understands.

"Oh! the beauty of the lightning's flash. The lightning which at twilight dashes like a naked sword across the firmament. This alone reveals the mystery of the universe in Tokyo's sullen sky. Between the thunder peals the lightning's flashes, juggler-like, suddenly appear and disappear, leaping from rift to rift of the far-sundered white goblin-shaped clouds.

"There is no fixed orbit for its path of light. Now it appears here, and then suddenly flashes its naked sword yonder in the most unexpected places. Now its color approaches a threatening purple, and then, quickly transformed to crystal clearness, it illuminates every nook and corner as far as the eye can see.

"In that mysterious moment I see one phase of the universe's fairest art. This marvelous art, not made by human hands, is revealed only to those who have conquered fear and love the beauty of the cosmos.

"In the presence of that electrical display the great city grows strangely silent. I rejoice as the lightning, unchanged from of old and unwearied, plays over the silenced city and its boasted culture, hurling its lovely light upon the earth. Standing quietly and alone on the hillside and lost in meditation regarding this juggler in the sky, the great city fades away and the lightning only becomes my close-bosomed friend."

In Nature's fiercest moods she fascinates him. "The tempestuous rain—I love it! How fine the feeling to walk with head erect, clad in a water-proof, through a raging gale that all but sweeps you off your feet. The while the rain comes pelting down like pounding bullets. Let the cowards all hide in their homes. As for me, with eyes intent, I will gaze enraptured on this climax of the sublime drama which nature stages.

"The floods roar as they twist and turn. The rivers raise the battle cry and rush over their banks. Riotous clouds sweep low. There is a bustle and hustle as men rush forth to strengthen the dikes. Nature reveals a tense mood and shows a sternness which cannot be despised.

"To men of the common mold and those addicted to indolence and ease the storm is a sort of lash in the hand of God. But to our young souls it is Nature rendering the supremest of symphonies. Blow! Oh, tempest, blow! Blow away the nation's effeminate morale. Those who cannot outride the storm are too soft to bequeath strong guts to the oncoming generations. Blow! Oh, tempest, blow! Blow and strengthen the nation's roots."

This ecstasy of the quest for reality leads him out into realms to which most men are not only total strangers, but where their feet falter. It fills him with an all-embracing cosmic consciousness. It creates in his soul a sense of kinship not only with the unseen, but with all that is seen.

"The whole creation is mine. My life penetrates to the heart of every created thing. In the kitchen it is one with the spirit of the fire, one with the spirit of the water, and one with the spirit of the blazing range. All things appeal to me. I am merged into everything. I can dwell with the soot in the chimney and find a peaceful place with the flea under the matted straw.

"Set free, I fly upward to the constellation of the Great Bear. I speed from star to star. Or I conceal myself in the depths of my loved one's dressing-mirror. As long as I love the whole creation I can travel about it with the utmost freedom.

"Both Mount Fuji and the Japanese Alps are but wrinkles on my brow. The Atlantic and the Pacific are my robes. The earth forms a part of my footstool. I hold the solar system in the palm of my hand. I scatter millions of stars across the heavens. The whole creation is mine. God threw it in when He gave me Christ."

To Kagawa every bush is a cathedral, every stone an altar, every task a sermon, every act a prayer, and every breath incense rising to God who waits to be worshiped everywhere.

"Stirred by the song of my comrade at work in the kitchen, I am moved to lift my voice in the same sweet melody:

Radiant with mercy,
Fragrant with love,
How beautiful are the
Footsteps of my Lord.

"My heart is gripped by that quiet tune. In the life of

our day, which lacks both brightness and fragrance, I think of the blessedness of following the beauteous footsteps of the Man of God and living this earthly life as one pressing toward the heights of holy living.

"No place of worship! No altar! Yet with this song my soul offers up its sincere worship to God. Out of the fullness of my heart the song arises. My blinded eyes become a fountain of tears. To God who stands in my very presence I lift up my voice in ecstasies of praise. My prayer is a song. My song is a prayer.

"My sanctuary opens the moment I put my hand to the broom. With the motion of the duster a song of praise ascends. My work is blessed by the choir which dwells within my soul. I am myself the father confessor. I alone am the choir. I alone am the audience. In the sanctuary of my heart the purple flame of the burning incense rises. God, quietly listening at the window of my soul, open heavenward, hears the song which I offer."

Kagawa has developed the technique of discovering and exploring God and of experiencing Him in such a vivid and vital way that God no longer dwells in the marginal recesses of his soul, but fills and illumines and dominates his whole conscious life.

If we put aside pressing cares and allow the life of the universe to whisper to our hearts, living becomes pure joy. Then the heart will be detached from illusions and worldly cares be overcome. Even in the midst of the most chaotic scenes there will be a stillness of soul which is undisturbable.

—Kagawa's *Meditations.*

XI

SOME CLOSE-UPS

THE UNENCUMBERED LIFE

I HATE THINGS WHICH ONLY CAUSE TROUBLE. I HAVE NO hankering to live a so-called civilized life. To the last let me be a child of nature. If the woods and owls, and the rabbits and barnyard fowls, pronounce their blessings upon me, my cup of life shall be full to the brim.

"There is nothing more exhilarating than to walk through the world unencumbered. If possessions abound there is a haunting fear that they may be stolen. If you are beautifully gowned you worry lest your garments be soiled. If you are high of rank you are anxious lest you be thrown down. If you pride yourself on being erudite, you are cut to the quick if some one makes light of you. Stripped to the skin! Stripped to the skin! That is the way to walk. . . ."

—KAGAWA'S *Meditations.*

XI

SOME CLOSE-UPS

KAGAWA IS AN ASCETIC IN HIS PERSONAL HABITS, BUT neither his face, with its sensitive mouth and expressive, soulful eyes, nor his genial bearing and ringing laughter, betray it. For him life is no futile, forlorn gesture. It teems with interest. It is an adventure that abounds in thrills. In his outlook and his attitude toward life he is the antitype of all that the ascetic has stood for in the past.

"In making life's journey we must not assume the mood of one who is crossing a sandy waste. Life must be made as enjoyable and smooth as possible.

"To go out of one's way to suffer and sigh, and purposely seek the perilous sandy stretches, is to tempt God. Since we are allotted but one life, its renunciation is not a matter of personal choice.

"It is by no means sinful to make our way through the world with as much peace of mind as possible, laughing as we go, maintaining an unhurried heart and with a pace that betokens time to spare. He who considers this a sin is a self-inflicted maniac.

"It cannot be that God has blundered so tragically in His making of our world. It is not wrong, in making our earthly journey, to lift our voices in praise to God and take a keen delight in life."

In build he is sturdy and stocky. Yet his physical frame is battered and broken with disease. He is half blind. His kidneys are affected. His lungs are infected. His heart constantly threatens to go on a strike. But with head unbowed and heart unafraid he faces life at the full and flings himself without stint into the fight, strong in the faith that he is immortal until his work is done.

"I will walk to the end of the last long mile and there, if fall I must, gladly will I fall. I have no desire to die on my bed. Will the summons to depart come to me on the high seas or speeding over the rails? That's as God wills. If I am but doing my utmost, all will be well.

"I have no sense of loneliness. The chariots of war which filled Jeremiah's vision are invisible to the eye of flesh, but they are constantly round about me. As long as I am with God even an army a million strong cannot put me to the sword. With this vision of the chariots of war a wonder-power sweeps down upon me from on high.

"I am one of those hopeless simpletons who, though living in this twentieth century, with its electrified civilization, still believes in the vision of chariots seen by Jeremiah.

"I still live in the midst of myths. Modern man has put them beyond the possibility of faith, but I find it impossible not to believe them. I do not live far removed from the age of myths. Nay, I live within these so called myths. Every day, as it were, I see visions of God's wondrous warring chariots."

His extravagances are those of faith and service. Here he knows no limit. His faith leaps over every obstacle and his service stops at no sacrifice. He is continually skirting the edge of personal poverty in his unceasing effort to relieve the needs of others.

He has received more than $100,000 in royalties from his books. Every cent of this has been spent on his three social settlements and in his work for the laborers and the peasants. All that he personally has to show for this relatively large income is a hampering debt loaded upon him by a defaulting publisher. He and Mrs. Kagawa limit their family budget to $40 a month for themselves and their three children. This is made to cover bare necessities. The remainder of the returns from his writings and books, totaling some years $10,000, all goes into the work for the poor and the winning of a freer, fuller life for those who toil.

"The wolf of poverty unceasingly pursues me—I who am harassed by the devil of disease. All too well do I know the terribleness of the tug of this wolf's tusk. Hence I am ever fleeing at a breakneck speed. I cannot tell how far I will make good my escape, but, having somehow succeeded until now, it seems probable that in the future, too, flight will be possible. Come on, O Wolf of Poverty! Come on! I will keep just one step ahead in this furious flight.

"Not that I do not feel fagged, at times, as a result of the desperateness of this distress; yet, I am grateful to God that it keeps me constantly on the alert. Money in a measure has been mine. When I saw, however, that most men were penniless its possession filled me with a sense of shame and I scattered it abroad. Thus, like the rest, I am closely pressed by the pursuing wolf of straitened circumstances. Still the suffering caused by the lack of money is easier to bear than the worry which accompanies its possession.

"If God but grants me strength to keep just one step ahead in the flight I shall continue my present course. When one is on one's mettle it is possible to keep very near to God. And since nearness to God is for me the greatest of all blessings, despite the frightfulness of this wolf, I will flee until I fall.

"As regards the far future, that is in God's hand. Here, blind as I am, though driven to bay by the wolf, with faith in God's guidance I will run through the dark to the uttermost of my strength. As long as I can make good my escape my life will be victory crowned."

Anomalous though it sounds, this disciple of poverty is one of the Empire's most generous givers. Some of his friends call him the modern hundred-handed Goddess of Mercy. His three settlements minister to multitudes. The labor and peasant movements draw heavily on his resources. Moreover, wherever he goes the hungry turn to him, and he feeds them. The naked appeal to him, and he clothes them. Repeatedly he returns to his home at the close of a bitter winter day minus his overcoat. It has been given to some shivering brother met along the way. The sick turn to him, and he provides for them. The unemployed knock at his door, and he takes them in, feeds them at his own table, and shelters them in his own home week on week.

Would his use of money meet the efficiency expert's test? Would Jesus' way meet that test? It is rumored that the reason some generous-minded Japanese men of wealth hesitate to underwrite Kagawa and his numerous projects is their fear lest his pace would soon drain them dry. The question as to whether men and women are worthy or unworthy is never raised. Hunger, nakedness, and want are the only appeals needed to move the heart and hand of this knight-errant who goes through life as God's spendthrift. He feels that the devil too long has had a monopoly on the world's spendthrifts and that it is only fair that God should have a few.

"I know the secret by which life can be made easy. If one lives modestly the problem of bread is not so difficult. Yet when the masses suffer as at present it is utterly out of the question for me to live on Easy Street.

"Like the gambler I wager everything before God. I stake everything I have for the Kingdom enterprise. Unless the grain of seed is sown it can never come back increased an hundredfold.

"The gambler chief in the Shinkawa slums, whom I well knew, hazarded his all. I do the same for a good cause. Whether it will mean nakednes or whether I win can only be known by a throw of the dice.

"I have staked my all; property, position, fame, everything has been staked for God. Heads or tails, which will it be? That's as God wills. It is this gambler's course which I pursue that keeps my purse so poor. The prophet Jeremiah called himself God's tippler. I will call myself God's gambler. For him I have wagered my last mite."

Among the lowly, as well as among those of high estate, he wears his $1.85 laborer's suit which fits him like a sack, but beneath this rough exterior men soon discover the shining armor of a soul that needs no outer embellishments.

"Sin, for the most part, forces itself in when a false note is struck. When pride is in the saddle, when one is over-confident, when one assumes an air of ignorance, when one pretends victory in defeat, these are the times when sin makes a raid on the soul.

"Adultery has its root in self-conceit. Burglary has its source in vanity. The murderer thinks that he alone is right. Falsehood and greed come from a desire to live out of keeping with one's station in life. These all come from the desire to live a double life and are impossible to the man who is satisfied to reveal his unadorned self in a straightforward, honest way.

"There is no deception about the illiterate man who simply passes as an illiterate. The man with no self-conceit does not commit adultery. He who does not exaggerate his own importance has no courage to commit murder, nor will he become infatuated with a woman who is enamored with him. The man who has no desire to make a vain display will neither rob nor covet.

"In a word, sin raises its head wherever there is a yearning to put on an imposing appearance. Sin of every description has its root in a fondness for display. The murder demon is always the captive of vanity. All adulterers are the object of the adoration of the self-conceited. Those who look lightly on appearance commit no sin. I was a child of vanity. I lived in the midst of vanity. But I rejoice that I have been liberated from it all."

For him the zest for high living does not seem to lose its glow. When for the sake of the physical and moral welfare of his children he reluctantly left the hut in the slums of Kobe and temporarily moved to one of the Tokyo suburbs, he did not forsake his simple, unostentatious ways. Within sight and sound of the mighty metropolis he built, with his own hands, a small Japanese house. The lumber for this home was salvaged from the temporary shacks erected to shelter the people following the great earthquake. Its total cost was $80. Boxes were fitted with legs and shelves and serve as chairs, tables, and bookcases.

In this tiny, rough wood cottage lives Tokyo's most world-renowned citizen. From this humble home there emanate dynamic influences that touch with molding power not only the Japanese Empire, but the ends of the earth.

"It can be said that the ideal way is to live so simply that one can, in all things, serve oneself. What freedom there is in the life where one lives in a hut of one's own building, installs a kitchen hearth made by his own hands, cooks vegetables of one's own raising, wears garments woven on one's own loom and in simplicity manages one's own affairs.

"In such a life one enslaves no one. Sets up no one as

king. He is himself both king and butler, artist and laborer. This indeed makes a simplified world. If one lives a life of this sort near to a pool encircled by friendly trees, and fellowships daily with the owls and baby foxes, the intolerable city with its multitudinous noises loses its lure.

"If it is impossible to carry out this ideal alone, it ought at least to be possible to guide one's family into a life approximating it; and not only one's immediate family; it ought to lie within the range of possibility to create an atmosphere in which the entire village would be satisfied to live on this simplified scale.

"Machinery offers no obstacles. It, too, can be made subordinate in a life where one is one's own master."

He refuses to be enslaved by a mass of minor matters that do not count, and spends his time and energy grappling with the great issues of life.

"One of the fearful things to which we are fated is to worry about a multitude of unnecessary matters. As soon as we arise, in comes the morning paper with its glaring headlines and narrations of facts which blow to atoms the morning's quiet.

"Its reading alone furnishes enough cause for driving civilized man mad. The reason this does not happen is his blasé attitude. If we seriously considered what we read it would be absolutely impossible to go on.

"Tolstoy said, 'Stop and think!' This is a deep philosophy. While civilization stands at the crossroads we are concerned with all kinds of unimportant things. The design of one's dress, the style of one's hair, the powdering of one's nose, how to paint one's face, the good or bad quality of one's toilet soap, the color of one's socks, the shape of one's shoes, what words to use, noting the shade of color on another's face, wasting time with the tradespeople who call at the back door, currying favor with one's neighbors, the fluctuation of the market, and other endless meaningless minutia."

Kagawa's espousal of the simple life is not a fad or a fancy. It is rooted in the deep-going principles of soul liberty and social justice. He wants to leave his soul unencumbered and unfettered in its climb to the heights. Moreover, he recognizes that luxury and display mean heavier burdens for other backs.

"Nothing causes so much trouble as even a taste of luxurious living. If the wind blows, you worry about the garden trees. If it rains, it is the ceiling that causes concern. Such minor matters as the hanging of a picture or the choice of paper for a wall consume a whole day. The dressing of the hair ruins half a day. Powdering the face wrecks the other half. Then, if that person dies young the sum and substance of her life becomes wall-paper, plus face-powder, plus a powder-puff.

"If by means of her own work she can get through life on such a basis, well and good, but after all who provides food for one who surrenders herself to wall-paper, face-paint and a powder-puff? Is it not true that unless she squeezes more than usual out of other people she would have no such reserve of time and money?"

Not simply in his outward life does Kagawa renounce much of the clutter that twentieth-century man, with his mania for things, burdens himself with, but he escapes ennui and satiation by finding thrills in the common things.

"Oh, to be a child once more! Cheerful, agile, interested in every passing thing, throwing each muscle into action, giving to grief, when it comes, only a moment's thought.

"The child speaks to the stars. It makes friends with the violet. It talks with the spirit of the pool. In the woods it makes comrades of the trees. The dragonfly, the butterfly, and the locust manifest toward it a special kindness. Such a child I would be once more!

"Why is it that with the advancing years the muscles harden, wrinkles burrow their way into the skin, interest in things wanes, and life becomes a succession of yawns?

"Forever I would be a babe. I would feel an eternal friendship for the raindrop, the camellia, the bleeding-heart and the flake of snow. As long as I have a yearning to be a child I will find delight in this earthly life. Forever I would be guileless. Forever I would be inquisitive. Truly only a child can enter into the Kingdom of God."

He keeps his mind mounting from height to height by thinking the thoughts of the great of all the ages. He is an insatiable reader. When studying at Princeton University he astonished his professors by presenting a list of forty-two books on the theory of evolution which he had read. Undeterred by his impaired vision, he still fellowships with sages and saints through their books.

"Fall has come again. The season which brings the joy of listening to the insects' call and hobnobbing in solitude and quietness with one's favorite author. There is no delight comparable to that of all alone, in fellowship with a friendly light, reveling in a book far into the night. It is like making one's way through deep mountain recesses. Books read under such conditions are never forgotten.

"It is my rule to read only books from which I seek instruction. I am too busy to read books simply for the purpose of sitting in judgment on the thought they present.

"The reading of books is like mountain-climbing. Even though one reads a book of meager content one's outlook is not enlarged. It may be said that only he who has scaled the Alps has really climbed a mountain. Unless one reads substantial books, books which take rank as authorities, the alluring autumn time will pass without any climbing records having been established.

"I want to tramp over the Alps of the world's thinking. As in mountain-climbing one scales peak after peak, so in the mountain ranges of thought there is a scaling of the highest peaks. I wait for autumn's revel, fully determined to scale the high mountain ranges of the history of human thought."

When threatened with total blindness and compelled to lie for months with bandaged eyes in a darkened room, he had hours when the far horizons were hid in mists and his career seemed to have come to an untimely close, yet through it all his far-visioned soul reveled in a light that does not shine on sea or land.

"'It's inconvenient, isn't it?' 'What?' 'Your blindness.' 'Yes, but it is inconvenient for people not to have wings, isn't it? If, however, they invent airplanes, these take the place of wings.'

"The same is true regarding the external eyes. If they go blind it is simply a matter of inventing internal sight. My God is light itself. Even though every outward thing is shrouded in darkness in the inner chamber of my soul, God's Eternal light shines on.

Burn! oh, thou inner light, burn!
Burn on, oh light, fed from the oil
That never fails.

"God will keep for me that little light forever burning. He himself is my light, and as long as He shines within I do not lament being compelled to sit out the long day in darkness.

"Health is gone! Sight is gone! But as I lie forsaken in

this dark room God still gives light. Pains that pierce the very fires of Hell itself sweep over me. Yet, even in the melting fires of hell, God's mercy, for which all of earth's manifold treasures would be an utterly inadequate exchange, still enfolds me.

"At the center of things there is a heart. On the yonder side of darkness there is light. Deprived of sight, I discern that light flooding in through the darkness.

"To me all things are vocal. Oh, wonder words of love! The bedding, the tears, the spittle, the perspiration, the vapor of the compress on my eyes, the ceiling, the matted floor, the voice of the chirping sparrow without, all are vocal. God and every inanimate thing speak to me. Thus even in the dark I feel no sense of loneliness."

During those long dark days unceasing prayer was the plummet with which he fathomed God's wonder ways. "Prayer continues! Prayer continues! Daily my prayer continues! Back of the blinded eyes prayer continues. Be the sky clouded or clear, my prayer continues.

"Given the gift of life, I must pray—pray for God's Kingdom, pray for the world. Simply because I am doomed to dwell in the dark is no excuse for allowing my soul to devote itself to self-centered musings.

"In the darkness I meet God face to face. In the darkness my soul is clothed in white raiment and, purified, ascends to the holy of holies, into the very presence of God. The darkness itself is a holy of holies of which no one can rob me.

"That's it! That's it! It is not I that believe in God. It is God who is bringing me to the birth. Here lies the reason for this long blindness. This is the purpose back of this wearisome confinement. I am being born, born of God. God has some great expectation regarding me. I must not give way to despair because of pain or sorrow. God is bearing me in his womb.

"A faint mental effort brings to the surface a dim consciousness which speaks as though in prophecy of a world to come. But even this cannot be relied upon. Unconscious though it seems, it is not unconscious. Consciousness there seems to be, but there is none. Here on this earth we live a life deep in the womb, embryonic, like the chick forming in the egg shell. The dawn is still far away. Let us for a while fold our wings, contract our knucklebones, close our eyes, and behold the Omnipotent's mighty work."

In those dark and seemingly hopeless hours his spirit moved clear-eyed and free in the higher reaches of life and discovered unutterable compensations.

"With the thought of comforting me, a friend remarked, 'Because so many things are waiting to be done you must find this long illness tedious.' I, however, was compelled to confess that I was not conscious of any sense of ennui. I realize that a lot of work is waiting. But work is not the purpose of my life. I am given life that I may live.

"It is impossible for me to stupidly moon away this present precious moment in boredom by idly thinking of tomorrow. My life is focused in this one moment. My present task is here and now to fellowship with God on this bed of pain.

"I am not thinking of tomorrow or the next day, nor even of this day's sunset hour. I am concerned only with being, this present moment, without any sense of tedium, with God. And for me constantly praising God for the joy of the moments lived with Him there is no such thing as tediousness."

Most ascetics brood over their weaknesses and sound the sad note of a runner who faints and falls in sight of the goal. This one, however, gathers strength and speed with the passing of the years and frankly glories in it.

"I, too, indulge in glorying. Even though I have nothing in which to glory around me, when I face my own soul I find innumerable reasons.

"I cannot refrain from glorying in the fact that from the day I first found God the power of evil within me has waned and the power of righteousness has waxed.

"If others glory in the fact that they have slaughtered their tens of thousands and distinguished themselves on the field of battle, I will glory in the fact that, being a weakling, I haven't the guts to kill even one single being.

"If there are those who glory in the frequency of their visits to the *demi-monde* quarters and of having soiled their souls with a thousand courtesans, I will face my soul with pride in the fact that because of lack of manliness, so called, I have known no woman but my wife.

"I have neither the courage to lie nor the mettle to possess myself of others' goods. I glory to myself that mine is a weak soul.

"Paul declared, 'When I am weak, then am I strong.' I rejoice that because I am infirm and wanting in virility I can glory in the power of God."

I FIND NO NECESSITY, WHATEVER, FOR PESSIMISM. HAVE I NOT strength in abundance to lay temptations low? Who says that the flesh has a mighty influence over the spirit? My experience is just the reverse. If I may be allowed a confession in which there is no deceit, I see no need for concealing the fact that I am surprisingly strong.

Why do the world's writers make their weakness the central theme of their writings? If there is literary merit in sincere confession, I will glory in my strength.

I confess that the urge toward holiness within me will not listen to the thought of reveling in momentary pleasures. Since I became God-possessed it has become impossible for me to commit my soul to wanton thoughts. I glory! I glory in the might of the Almighty who dwells within me.

—KAGAWA'S *Meditations.*

XII

THE COMRADE OF THE ROAD

THE CHILD'S MYSTIC POWERS

My little laddie is a poet. He sings off a lot of meaningless words and joyously declares it is a song of his own composing. He makes a pillow of his daddy's arm and says that he can hear the sound of a song singing up out of its depths. Such and other poetical sayings he rattles off.

He is just three years and eight months. Even though I do not have access to Maeterlinck's hero of *The Blue Bird*, my laddie is an efficient guide into the land of the soul. He leads me also into the happy land where cares are forgotten. He is my guide into the world of magic mirrors.

Christ's saying, "Whosoever shall not receive the Kingdom of God as a little child, he shall in no wise enter therein," is indeed right and reasonable.

Even though you reverence and hold in awe the vapid nonsense put forward by old men and call it ethics and morals and what not, yet the ideals which bring manhood to perfection will not be reached through these in a thousand years. Only when one becomes a babe filled with juvenescent, ever-expanding strength will it be possible to see for a certainty the energetic processes of manhood marching on to its perfect consummation.

—Kagawa's *Meditations*.

XII

THE COMRADE OF THE ROAD

THE YEAR OF KAGAWA'S BIRTH MARKED THE APPEARANCE in a far-distant city of a dark-haired, brown-eyed lassie who was destined to play an outstanding rôle in the colorful life which lay in the womb of his future. Her parents bestowed on this babe the prophetic name of "Spring."

Like Kagawa, she was born in a home of plenty. Soon after her advent, however, the family fortunes took an adverse turn. The result was that Miss Spring, as soon as she had finished the primary school, at the age of fifteen, was compelled to help meet the family budget by working as a domestic servant.

Reverse followed reverse and the family was finally forced to leave Yokosuka, the beautiful city by the sea, and they moved to Kobe in search of employment. Here Miss Spring entered service in the book-binding department of a publishing concern at a daily wage of six cents. She early gave evidence of possessing more than ordinary ability and after one year, at the age of eighteen, she was put in charge of the thirty girls in this department, directing and overseeing their work. Her wages gradually rose to twelve cents a day. For nine long years she shared the monotonous life and the wearing, wearying work of these factory girls.

This establishment was under Christian management and a local pastor came regularly to conduct services for the employees. Miss Spring encouraged the girls to attend these meetings, but her interest was wholly of a professional nature. She was deeply concerned about the workers, whose lot she shared, and hoped that attendance at these services might open the way for some ray of cheer and sunshine to break in upon the galling monotony of their drab and colorless existence.

Her own heart, however, was in open rebellion to all that the speaker said. She had witnessed her aunt pass through a period of prolonged and intense suffering which ended in an agonizing death. Every memory of that experience deepened the conviction that no God of Love would or could permit such pain.

Kagawa was at that time attending the Kobe Theological Seminary and to him was assigned the task of periodically going down to this publishing-house to teach the girls Gospel songs. One evening when Miss Spring was passing through the Shinkawa district a crowd of people gathered at a street corner attracted her attention. Inquiry revealed the fact that a street meeting was in progress. Curiosity caused her to stop and listen.

There was no harmony in the singing. The hearers were a motley group—poverty-stricken laborers, apprentices, diseased street women, and beggars in filthy rags. The group of Christians who did the singing was made up of mail-carriers, factory workers, staggering old men, invalid beggars, and ex-prostitutes crippled with disease.

While she waited, a young man walked briskly up and joined the group. He was dressed in a faded suit and shirt and carried a New Testament in his hand. When she saw his face she caught her breath and murmured to herself, "Why, that's the young man who comes and teaches the girls to sing!"

During the summer vacation Kagawa took the regular evangelist's place as preacher at the plant. Even at this early stage in his career he was a flaming apostle of love.

Utterly ignorant of the battle which was raging in the heart of the head of the binding department, he made the love of God the central theme of his preaching. He showed that love and suffering are inseparable. He traced the redemptive work of pain and sacrifice through the ages. He stressed the fact that only in those who go through the school of suffering does character come to its finest and fairest flower.

In the heat of those summer evenings he grappled with the problem which was preventing his most potential hearer from giving the teachings of Christ a hearing, solved it to her satisfaction, and awakened in her an urge to give herself to a life of love. She became a regular attendant at his slum services, and on December 21, 1913, in the hut church in Shinkawa, was baptized by Dr. Meyers into the Christian faith.

She was now a woman of twenty-five and the faith which had found entrance into her heart became an aggressive, dynamic force in her life. She organized a Sunday school for the girls in the publishing-house. Not satisfied with this, she toiled all day in the bindery and at night assisted Kagawa with his street meetings in the slums. In order to avoid gossip, she took the precaution of being accompanied by her younger sister in these excursions to Shinkawa. Yet the fact that she—a woman—helped a single man hold street meetings in so disreputable a section caused a sensation and brought down upon her disfavor and persecution from her fellow workers in the plant.

In Japan it has been an immemorial custom for the parents to choose the life mate for their children and make the marriage arrangements. This sounds strange to Western ears, but in practice this system produces as many happy homes as the freer ways of the West. These two

eased prostitutes, and even mental defectives were given shelter for shorter or longer periods, with no one but her to minister to them. Her husband's strict vegetarian principles also created problems in the kitchen.

Yet none of these things seemed to her insuperable. She threw herself into the work of the settlement. She visited in the homes, nursed the sick, helped the new babies make their début, mothered the children, was the counselor and comforter of the mothers in all their problems and perplexities.

Every night she assisted in the meetings on the street. A Buddhist sect, stirred to action by Kagawa's example, started an opposition street preaching campaign. Shinkawa, always keen for a fight, flocked to the new banner and left the Christian group facing defeat. Mrs. Kagawa, ever resourceful, mounted a near-by cart and began to speak. Some one in the opposition camp raised the cry, "A woman! A woman! A woman preacher!" At this the crowd surged back to see and hear this new wonder, and the day was won.

Circumstances had deprived her of a higher education. But she was unwilling to yield the palm to circumstances. From six to seven in the morning and again from five to six in the evening Kagawa was giving instruction to two ambitious workingmen in mathematics, geometry, algebra, and kindred subjects. She joined the group. Moreover, in order to become efficient in the work to which she was devoting herself she spent her forenoons at the Kobe Woman's Bible School, studying the Bible and related subjects.

Her mettle is further shown by the step she took when her husband went abroad for study. She was now a mature woman. Yet she matriculated with girls her junior by many years in the Bible Training School for Women, at

Yokohama, studied there for three years, and graduated. After Kagawa's return from America he started a night school as one of the features of his slum settlement. Mrs. Kagawa enrolled as one of the students of this school. In season and out of season she climbed the rugged road to intellectual and cultural self-realization.

When a dispensary was added she took up nursing and cared for all kinds of filthy and contagious cases. In the course of this work she contracted trachoma of a virulent type and for many months was threatened with total blindness. Her sight was saved, but she still bears the marks of this dread disease and is constantly handicapped by it.

When her husband was imprisoned because of his connection with the Kobe dockyard strike she carried on in his stead. She had full charge of the two dispensaries connected with the settlement. She took the oversight of the "Friends of Jesus Society," an organization similar to the Franciscan order which Kagawa had launched for the purpose of recapturing the spirit of brotherhood which characterized the early Christian community. This society sets up peace, purity, piety, labor, and service as its five fundamentals and strives to demonstrate Jesus' way of life in terms of life and action.

She provided breakfast for from ten to fifteen people every morning and met from fifty to sixty visitors every day. She read hundreds of letters daily and saw that replies were sent. There were continuous consultations with the officials of the labor union, and measures adopted to keep up the morale of the striking workers.

When Kagawa became immersed in the work of the labor movement and there seemed a danger that he would lose his passion for the poor, she devoted herself with increased eagerness to befriending and helping the poverty-stricken people around her. She organized the "Kobe Wide

Awake Women's Society." This organization made self-culture and service for others its goal. It had a membership of five hundred workingwomen and published a monthly magazine for mothers.

She is the author of two small volumes, one dealing with the life of factory girls, the other with conditions in the slums. Through articles for the press she helped her husband put the slum on the nation's conscience. One of these dealt with the illicit prostitution which poisoned the life of old and young in Shinkawa. This angered one of the masters of the women victims of this system. He rushed to the hut and, finding her alone, gave her a good beating.

Her rôle has not been an easy one. Yet in looking back over the years she declares that there have been rich compensations—the faithfulness of those who have been won for the new life; the devotion of the children—when sick they called for her rather than for the doctor, that they might look into her face and hear her pray.

Out of Shinkawa have come twice-born women who have cast a redeeming light over the whole of that dark district. One of these was the wife of a poverty-stricken bean-curd peddler. The son was a gambler, his parents encouraging him in it. When he began to attend the slum Sunday school they were up in arms. But the change that came over the lad touched the mother's heart. She followed him to the chapel and to Christ, and has never ceased to hold high the torch of contagious Christian example. The son today is an earnest, effective pastor.

Mrs. Kagawa has given herself with crusading zeal to the work of redeeming the slums and creating a better community for men and women to live in. Still, it is her conviction that the home is woman's most challenging and fertile field. The making of good homes and the rearing of good children she feels to be the safest and surest way of rebuilding the social order. The home training of children she considers of first importance in solving such major problems as social purity, justice as between man and man, race relations, and war. If in the creative atmosphere of a Christ-centered home the plastic child mind is inoculated with right ideas regarding life in all its various relations, the coming of the Kingdom is assured.

Kagawa's way has been uncharted, often perilous, and richly rewarding, but eternity alone will reveal how much he owes to this unassuming, self-effacing, heroic comrade of the road.

Two streams of life. One issued forth from Awa. The other emerged from the city by the sea. Both flowed from their far separated and distant sources, met, merged, revolutionized the life of Shinkawa and are mighty forces in the Christian infiltration of every phase of Japan's life. Was it simply a coincidence? Merely the work of fixed law? The chance outworking of blind fate?

XIII

SOME KAGAWAGRAPHS

I AM IMPELLED TO LOVE. THIS IN ME IS AN INSTINCT STRONGER and mightier than the desire to be loved. From seven until seventeen I was in continuous anguish because of a yearning for the love of others. Now that I have passed life's fortieth milestone, the urge to love is by far more compelling.

My concern is not that of being loved by my wife and children. On the contrary, I have a passionate desire to love them. In a word, the parent instinct has awakened within me. It appears that the function of physical reproduction combined with a psychological instinct makes me conscious of an inner impulse to forget myself in my love for others. When I love my children I am conscious of the highest of all happiness. When the children are not around I am of all men most lonely. I want to love! This may be called my passion to live creatively.

—KAGAWA'S *Meditations*.

XIII

SOME KAGAWAGRAPHS

THESE PARAGRAPHS DO NOT REPRESENT ANY CONTINUITY of thought. They were chosen at random from Kagawa's *Meditations* and other writings and are brought together here because they serve as open windows into the range of his thinking and help to give the measure of the man.

I. MISCELLANEOUS

"Time is an unfathomable secret to him who is always in a rush. Time is a strange solver of the problems which afflict mind and heart. Time is a comforter. Time is a friend.

"Think not that the darkness will never end. When the day dawns the sun will greet you from the east. The storm will not last forever. When it has passed a great calm will come.

"Nothing is so strange as time. Time brings growth toward a goal. Time transforms the child into a man. Time buries tyrants.

"In tune with time the sick are healed, the broken-hearted recover, the poignant pain caused by failure is cured, and the sprouts of wheat that lie buried under the snow prepare for future growth.

"Time is the mother of invention. Time is the father of discovery. O soul, fret not thyself! In the day of thy distress meditate on the way in which time deals with you and wait."

"It often happens that those who have cut their way through hardships, over-elated with their success, set up their own strong wills as a criterion and have no sympathy for the adversities of the very weak.

"Again, those who are in the midst of trouble have no leisure to think of others and leave the afflicted to their fate. Moreover, many never having tasted hardship are unable to sympathize with the distress of others.

"To have overcome hardship and not be puffed up; to be in the throes of adversity and be unafraid; not to shrink from difficulties when they appear in the offing—these things are possible only to those who are immersed in the great love of the cosmos."

"Unless one educates his emotions they deteriorate to the level of the beasts. The need of educating the feelings does not seem to have occurred to present-day educators. The reason Confucius stressed the social code of etiquette and music was wholly in the interest of educating the emotions.

"The emotions cannot be educated simply through art. I am not opposed to æsthetic and musical education. However, the unique way of teaching humor, seriousness, mental mettle, composure, gentleness, and benevolence is to provide means of contact with nature and with God. Until God is recovered, the emotions of the rough-mannered men of our day cannot be restored to a healthy state."

"One must not go astray regarding fate. Law is not fate. Law can be utilized to one's advantage.

"It must not be thought that the destiny of this world is fixed. Those who look only at the surface of things often fall into this error. But the power of the inanimate world, the dynamics of mechanical might, and all power manifested through motion are not blind. They conform to an orderly law. More than that they will conform to an inner power, to an inner purpose, namely to the mysterious purpose which man possesses and they can be altered in whatever way he wills.

"Thus, as long as man does not abandon the high ideals and purposes hidden within himself he will never be caught in the net of fate. Dynamite crushes the granite rock. Purpose conquers fate. One must not take a gloomy view of fate so-called."

"There is a saying, 'The semblance of a man but the heart of a beast.' It is difficult for me to approve of this saying. In studying the monkey or the fox I cannot find that they possess a more warped nature than man. Where does the monkey, like many nations, have prostitutes that number tens of thousands?

"In reading Hartman's *A Study of the Monkey* I was amazed to learn that the gorilla is a faithful monogamist. In the face of the fact that the monkeys which inhabit the forests of the Torrid Zone are monogamistic, is it not true that many men are polygamists?

"I have not heard of monkeys consuming liquor at the rate of hundreds of millions of gallons a year, as many peoples do. Even the lion, in facing a feast, knows when enough is enough.

"Among carnivorous animals it is said that the leopards are the worst natured, but even they do not indulge in killing off twelve million human beings and wounding an additional twenty million in the brief space of four years and eight months.

"If the wolf or the wild boar were to hear the words 'The semblance of a man but the heart of a beast,' great indeed would be their wrath! In their behalf let me suggest that henceforth the saying be, 'The semblance of an animal but the heart of a man.' This more nearly expresses the truth."

"If there are living beings with active intellects inhabiting the planet Mars, I believe that physically they are pretty much similar to the race of men dwelling upon this earth.

"Granted that the principles which govern the universe are boundless in number, yet those governing life itself are not so multiform. Moreover, although it may seem marvelous—and marvelous it certainly is—the trends of evolution which differ somewhat in the various species are, up to a certain stage, similar.

"Even though there be a vast distance between the earth and Mars, in all likelihood the principle of life which runs through both of these planets is one and the same. Also, doubtless, the trends of evolution here and there are not mutually different.

"This is not simply a flight of imagination on my part. A study of the trends of the many different forms of life reveals the fact that there is one fundamental principle common to all. This principle transcends all space. And life, in all probability, makes no distinction between our planet and Mars."

"Happy is he who knows how to toil contentedly within the range of his possibilities. Where one daringly attempts what for him is impossible he runs the hazard of essaying to sail through the skies without wings. Adventure is all right. But adventure which exceeds ability leads to catastrophe.

"When a heavy burden must be borne, it is unreasonable for him who can carry only a hundred pounds to attempt a load of twice that weight. There is no particular need for him to shoulder it alone. Why not call a friend to his aid and the two of them tackle it? Or, if it can be transported by machine power—well and good. My brother! don't grow impatient. If you cannot budge it, why not bring the lever? Let us do all that lies within the range of possibility.

"Simply because a thing cannot be done now does not signify that it can never be done. Who, twenty years ago, dreamed of the airplanes which soar through the skies of our day? Or who, in his farthest flights of fancy, conceived of the radio ten years ago?

"Let us with tranquil mind and a deliberate soul take up our task! Let us do what we can! What cannot be done in this generation may well be put off until the next! This to me is not a question of fate, but of circumstances. I am satisfied with the possibilities which have been allotted to me."

"Let us lift up our voices and laugh, laugh with hearty laughter. Let us laugh at idols of every description. Laughter must be our weapon in overthrowing vanities of any and every kind.

"The idols of Greece fell before Aristides' laughter. The idols of Rome were made valueless before the laughter of Lucian. Before Cervantes' laughter the knights of feudalism were treated like somnambulists walking about with tin pans on their heads. Before the laughter of Voltaire the position of the autocratic class in France was undermined and a new age came to the birth.

"Laugh! Laugh boisterously! Weeping is one device, but laughter is another resource. Laughter is the outcome of violent change. Let him laugh who wants to break up the *status quo*. Dante caused the world to smile and laid the foundations for a great religious reformation. Laugh! Laugh! Laugh at those who worship the host of intrenched idols of our day, idols in whom there is no help! More powerful by far than the pistol, mightier by much than dynamite is the power of laughter."

"There are times when one is tempted to think that the world is a mass of contradictions and discords, errors and evils, a place not fit to live in.

"At such a time it behooves one first of all to quietly reflect on the state of one's health, one's mental mood, one's circumstances and one's work. When the fulcrum of one's own inner center of gravity loses its equilibrium the world's uglinesses assume an exaggerated appearance and cast a dark shadow across the soul.

"It must be remembered that not every shadow imaged in one's own heart reflects a world-wide distress. If disease is healed, health is restored, mental agony is removed, circumstances take a turn for the better and the burden of one's work is somewhat eased, the world's dark shadow, which had settled on one's spirit, all unawares lifts and disappears.

"Having lived thus far, the rest of life's journey ought not to be impossible. Just a little more effort! Nay, better still, face forward and energetically strive to rectify the world's wrongs. One must not take too gloomy a view of the world."

"Many indeed have been my days of solitude. Bereft of my parents in childhood, from my earliest days I have experienced but little of the love of kith and kin. A whole year I spent alone in a duel with death in the hospital of a lonely fishing village. I passed six long months alone on the tablelands of Utah.

"I have thus had ample opportunity to think about solitude. If when the lonely times come one pours mind and heart into study or gives oneself to passionate prayer, the sense of loneliness entirely disappears. When one neither studies nor prays, neither works nor meditates, and one's mental state is not properly poised, all sorts of erroneous obsessions harass the mind and a desperate feeling of loneliness sweeps in upon the soul. Let him who would conquer loneliness strive for mental poise."

"For him who is too busy, even the opportunity to listen to the voice of conscience is lost. The reason the cities teem with delinquent youth is because the child is no longer given an opportunity to reflect.

"The prevalence of homicidal insanity in America, where the machine civilization has made its greatest strides, is the same phenomenon as the growth of juvenile delinquency. The fact that modern man, cut off from nature and with no opportunity to reflect, abandons religion has its root in the same cause.

"If one speaks of reflection there are people, not a few, who smile. When I remarked to an American young lady that the women of her nation ought to learn the art of quietness, she replied with a cynical laugh. To quiet one's soul relieves the strain of the nerves, enables one to steer clear of mistaken judgments, and makes one's path plain.

"Reflection is practicing the art of listening to the voice of God. When this becomes a lost art, religion loses its reality and is doomed."

"In recent years there have arisen in the West those who have a very high regard for the religions of India. Those religions make negativism their essential element.

"It is not without reason that the life of the West,

which is progressing to the point where everything is made transient and which is satiated as a result of the World War, should be influenced to excess by the negative thought of the Indian faiths.

"It goes without saying that a negativism which insures safety is a far greater blessing than a positivism which leads to ruin. At the same time the inconsistent negative life which, while denying the actual still clings to it, must sooner or later be changed to a Mahayanaism which is grounded in affirmation.

"Simply from the standpoint of logic I believe that before espousing the negative life it is necessary to swing over from the denial of a carnalism which contends for place and power and pleasure to a positivism which is based on reflection and on an awakening in which the conscience is the ruling factor. Life transcends both negation and affirmation and bids us venture forth to the ideal world."

"There are no frontier lines in the realm of the spirit. Buddha is neither an Indian nor a Japanese. He belongs to the world of the spirit. The same is true of Christ. He was born in Judea, but He is not a Jew. He belongs to the whole wide world. Nay, he belongs to the universe.

"Are there boundary lines in Euclid or in geometry? Are there countries great or small in the world of electrical engineering? In the realm of knowledge and in the world of supreme values there is no question of boundaries, either narrow or broad.

"We must not build boundaries in the world of the soul. Japanese loyalty is something to be grateful for, but it is futile to advocate conquest in the realm of the spirit. I rejoice that the Japanese are conscious of their national heritage. There is no necessity of being over-imbued with Westernism. But I oppose the erecting of boundaries in the realm of truth and making distinctions in our love for men on the basis of the color of their skin. The soul transcends national boundaries; it takes no note of color or of race. The soul is an internationalist."

"I believe in prophecy regarding the destiny of the human race. Kepler prophetically designated the various orbits of the planets belonging to the solar system. Mendeléeff, basing his premises on the periodic groupage of the atom, predicted the discovery of new chemical elements. These predictions were fulfilled.

"There are also many prophecies regarding human conduct which prove true. That the evil perish and the righteous are finally victorious even the ordinary man recognizes. Some forms of prophecy regarding a decomposing civilization invariably come true. The prophets of Israel from ancient times foretold the downfall of their nation and their prophecies were fulfilled.

"If we investigate the tendency of history and project that trend into the future, the prophecy as to what must result cannot necessarily be called unscientific. To the pure conscience the future of civilization is indicated with a special sort of clearness.

"I believe in prophecy. To a conscience polished clear as crystal the destiny fixed for the wicked and that which awaits the righteous can, without much difficulty, be recognized by the angle at which they respectively tend."

"Whenever one returns to the city from nature's fair domain the conviction comes, with ever-increasing force, that modern civilization has to an absurd degree reached an impasse. Life has become convenient. It moves forward on a grand scale, but it is undeniable that gradually simplicity and the warm human touch are fading away.

"In saying this I by no means repudiate our machine civilization. Yet to me one teacup laboriously fashioned by the human hand is far more to be desired than half a dozen which are machine made. No matter how great its splendor, the product of the machine when it reaches a certain point creates a sense of satiety. However, things made with human hands, warped though their shape may be, hold the attention with an ever-increasing sense of satisfaction.

"The cities built in the Middle Ages lack the conveniences which characterize a modern city, yet in each and every stone and in each and every brick there is a human intimacy which captures the heart and makes you keenly conscious of an inexpressible friendliness.

"Thirty thousand is the right population for a city. When it goes beyond that I am haunted by a hankering to raze it to the ground. Modern man should be less grasping and adopt a simpler mode of life."

" 'Busy, busy!' says the woman as she shuts herself up in the rear of the house and sews away on finery she will wear, at the most, not more than three days during the year. Business men there are who repeat the refrain, 'Busy, busy,' as they rush to and fro between their offices and the establishments where their illicit lovers live.

"Military men take up the tune, 'Busy, busy,' as they care for their cannon and polish their guns. Students keep saying, 'Busy, busy,' as they sit up all night to prepare for examinations—and forget everything when the tests are over.

"The liquor dealer's bustle keeps the brothel-keeper busy. The brothel-keeper's busyness makes the physician busy. The physician's rushing keeps the chauffeur on the go. The chauffeur's activity in turn makes the liquor-dealer busy. Thus the ever-revolving circle turns round and round. Without any ideals, without any aspirations, this living corpse obtrudes itself around the earth.

"If this can be called a living social order, then the fire-wheels of hell in perpetual motion are a symbol of a perfect society. No marvel that the desire to seek God dies in such a society. The window through which God would invade a life so superficial and so completely absorbed in the present has been closed.

"God would simply be a nuisance in a capitalistic society and in an age where materialism has become the accepted norm of life. Thus in this whirl-about life it is necessary to put Him out of the way. If God comes in, the motion of this whirligig world would come to a stop. Life with God means an end of this merry-go-round existence and to live instead for things of the highest value."

"There are those who pour out curses on the machine. That is a mistake. The machine is not a thing to be cursed. If it is utilized as a medium for the expression of love for others, the machine is a magnificent creation.

"The evil arises when the machine is taken advantage of for individual profit. If love is made the basic force and factor in the utilization of machinery, no one ought to complain. For this reason I say curse not the machine.

"If the machine becomes monopolistic, let the community affected by its monopoly reverse the situation by taking control of it. To me the facts are simple. Even the machine was invented by God through the use of human brains as a blessing for mankind. I do not fear it."

II. Science

"For me science is a perfect art. The thought of there being a conflict between science and religion has never entered my mind. Give me an ever-deepening knowledge of science. Through this I will know more about the universe. A better understanding of the universe will give me a better understanding of myself. Knowing myself better, I will know God better.

"To say that religion conflicts with science is to say that science conflicts with oneself. Are not all things for our advantage? Not only so. Are not all things for the advantage of God who moves within us? The God who moves within is the same God who moves without. I see God in science which flashes in upon my mind like an art."

III. The Social Order

"The criminals whom I have known are most of them sick folk. Not only are they the prey of either physical or mental disease, but they grew up in a diseased society. Some of them are under the curse of their heredity, and some under the curse of undernourishment. Some are cursed by the homes in which they were born; some by their life in the slums. Some are suffering because of the curse which society inflicts upon them.

"I would like to convert all the prisons of our day into hospitals. Yet first of all it would be necessary to put the present curse-spreading society itself into such a hospital. Society today is a mentally defective invalid.

"The banks, the army, the tobacco shops, the saloons, the prostitute quarters, the geisha houses, the newspapers —do not all of them show symptoms of a diseased mentality? Society itself, today, has a criminal tendency. It is a self-caused lunatic. God and His cure alone can heal it."

"In Greek mythology there is a story of the gods punishing a man by depriving him of his shadow. It is a tragedy when what ought to be is in actuality wanting. For those who strive to really understand the meaning of life it is disagreeable to have forcibly withheld even that which can be dispensed with.

"In modern life those deprived of their shadows are the miners who spend their years in the bowels of the earth, the factory girls who toil through the night hours, and all women who are the tools of vice which in manifold forms reigns and riots under the cover of darkness.

"They are not only deprived of their shadows, but of their rest. The sun flees from them. Sleep deserts them. Thus human beings are condemned to a strange sort of life, utterly unthinkable for either plants or animals.

"It is only natural that those from whom the sun flees, and whom sleep deserts, should bring forth indigent offspring, a poetry flavored with insomnia, and a philosophy and an art that grope in the dark."

"In the realm of life there develops immediately a tendency to become a parasite on life's parent growth. The same is true of men. Those who are a little clever consider the parasitic life their right. Of this modern capitalism is the most conspicuous example.

"It is not, however, limited to capitalism. In every age the parasitic life makes its appearance in ever-changing forms. There is but one way to correct this tendency—that is to take a faithful attitude toward the main current of life.

"Those in ancient Israel who took a faithful attitude toward life's main stream were called prophets. These prophets, making God their criterion, criticized their age and mercilessly rebuked the wayward way of the masses.

The age will never come when prophets can be dispensed with in the religious world."

"I discover a strange note in Paul's writings. In his letter to the Romans he teaches that we are the possessors of the universe.

"To the Corinthians also he writes, 'Therefore, let no man glory in men. For all things are yours. Whether the world, or life, or death, or things present, or things to come, all things are yours.' Again he says, 'having nothing, yet possessing all things.'

"The fact that he claims the ownership of all things constantly compels me to think more profoundly and to stand amazed at the far-reach of his spiritual insight.

"Is there any way to an understanding of the nature of real ownership except by making God known among men? The thing of consuming interest regarding this question is that to Paul, who owned nothing, there came back the ownership of the whole wide world.

"Unless the private ownership of property, as well as the communistic system, return to Paul's teaching they will both ultimately come to naught."

IV. Nature

"If we think for a long time concerning any material object, we discover that things also possess an individuality. The brazier by the study table, with its friendly fire that spits and spurts, yes, even the charcoal-container by its side, speak with manifold meaning to the master of the house.

"Their shape, their color, their luster, the materials of which they are made, the place of their production, their maker, those whom they have served, the sequence of their journeyings to and fro, the events which have transpired around them, a host of such facts come one after the other thronging, crowding into the mind.

"Or the oblong brazier on the kitchen floor with its deep-cut scars and its many mars relates the family history with its sacred meaning. In short, the oblong brazier with the passing of the years has taken on a personality.

"For this reason, if we see a man's belongings we know what manner of man he is. If we enter the study of one whose things are gathered from a wide range of interest and are synthetically arranged we know exactly the lay of his mind.

"Just as human beings impart to things a human touch, so things exert a tremendous influence on men and women. That a gorgeous color scheme irritates men's minds and one of tasteful tones calms their souls is a fact well known.

"As I sit in the presence of these ever-silent inanimate things and ponder in this fashion, their boundless personalities in a multitude of forms draw near to me. As long as these mute friends exist I shall never know loneliness."

"I am passionately fond of the pouring rain. I do not love inclement weather, but I revel in the change. If you worry lest your clothing get wet, your thought is centered on umbrella and raincoat and what not. But if you face out into the storm, expecting a soaking, rain is refreshing beyond expression.

"Oh, the joy of feeling that you are in nature's bosom as, unburdened by an umbrella, wrapped in a water-proof, barefooted, you go splash, splash, stepping on over the solid soil. The earth beneath your feet shines as beautifully as though it had been polished with a luster-producing polish. The while you lap up the sweet drops of rain that fall on your face and scurry down your cheeks.

"The raindrops, leaping down from a height of many thousand feet, caper around your head and shoulders as though they were throbbing with life. In these drops of rain that come dancing down one senses a love that's aflame. Oh, the joy that thou shouldst find delight in me and cuddle down on my shoulders! The raindrop's limpid form is unsurpassingly lovely. The rain is my comrade. Nothing equals the pleasure of walking, umbrellaless and free through the pelting, pouring rain."

V. Art

"I do not necessarily disapprove of art for art's sake. I take off my hat to the deep devotion which sacrifices everything for the sake of beauty. However, hitherto, art for art's sake has advocated only the beauty centered in the senses and has given scant attention to the beauty centered in the soul. It has thought of the beauty of the individual and failed to consider the beauty of the group.

"Sense-centered beauty tends toward carnal pleasures, and individual beauty falls into selfishness. Therefore, among those who go in for art for art's sake and pursue beauty only, there are those who mistake selfish hedonism for art for art's sake.

"Eternal beauty is realized only through the purification of the life of the whole man. I do not repudiate beauty which is sensed through the senses, but this is not the whole of beauty. It is one of the essential elements of eternal beauty that it have its home in the soul.

"Beauty evolves. As long as one's own face only is beautiful and one's neighbor's defiled, only half of beauty has come to earth. The effort to beautify the face of one's neighbor goes by the name of morality. It must not be forgotten that in the life of the whole man morality also constitutes one of the essentials of art."

"Nothing is so curious as courtesy. Why do we bow? Why do we shake hands? Why do we pay attention to our personal appearance and regulate our manners according to rules? A moment's thought makes it all seem futile. Yet why do men indulge in this seemingly useless behavior?

"There is a profound reason. It is an effort on man's part to attain beauty. Wherever there is an absence of beauty there is a hidden sense of shame. This shame-mentality issues forth out of the instinct for beauty. The young maiden's bashfulness springs from her intense efforts toward beauty.

"Man's instinct spontaneously strives to dispense with whatever lacks beauty. When this beauty instinct emerges as respect, as friendship, as sociability, and as other psychological and moral behaviors, it takes the form of various courtesies which may at first seem superfluous.

"So long as the demand for beauty exists, so long will courtesy continue. Man's mode of life changes with each passing age. Accompanying this, the beauty types of muscular activity and the formalities which center attention on beauty will change. But courtesies which have beauty as their goal will never cease."

"Those who advocate art for art's sake are right. Man must make beauty one of the goals of his life. This is a part of his instinctive heritage.

"Beauty, however, must not be limited to the senses. For the purpose of life there is a variety of beauty. Virtue betokens the beauty of the soul. Therefore there are times when sense-centered beauty must give way to the beauty of the soul. By this I mean that there are times when partial beauty must give way to beauty full-blown, when sense-centered beauty must yield to beauty centered in life.

"Beauty is not blind. A beauty which can be thought of as being blind antedates the emergence of the soul. True beauty always grows simultaneously with the growth of the soul."

"Absolute beauty has two possible meanings. There is God-like beauty. There is also the surpassing beauty of the soul, built up within given limits and under certain circumstances.

"There is no greater beauty than these and there is no true beauty aside from these. That is to say, the beauty of the soul and the beauty of God are the two absolutes in the realm of beauty.

"God's beauty lies far beyond the possibilities of man's power to attain. Human standards for beauty change with changing conditions. Thus even the facial beauty of an attractive woman depends on how it is viewed. Sense-centered beauty, therefore, cannot be called absolute beauty.

"In order to preserve sense beauty as genuine beauty it is absolutely necessary to look at it from a new angle, with the soul as the medium. Then for the first time is it given a beauty that approaches the imperishable.

"There is no beauty apart from the soul. Beauty must be looked at with two sets of eyes, the eyes of sense and the eyes of the soul. When the image of these two sets of eyes blends, then and then only is a full-orbed beauty realized."

VI. Sin

"Sin! Oh, what a hateful word! The simple sound of it causes me to shudder. Sin destroys all things. It denies all things. It is darkness. It is destruction. It is death.

"What, then, is meant by sin? Everything estranged from God is sin. All behavior which simply skims the surface of things, takes cognizance of only a part and neglects the whole, takes thought of only the passing moment and is concerned with the senses only, is sin.

"He who sends his roots deep down into life, who makes the absolute the highest value and trudges the upward trail with eternity in his soul, has broken with sin. In other words, sin is that which has fallen away from life, from the absolute and from the eternal.

"Murder is a sin because it is a denial of life. Adultery is sinful because it is estranged from that which is eternal in love. Lying is wrong because it violates the absolute character of truth. Stealing is sinful because it is a parasite on life's instinctive urge to grow. Greed is sinful because it destroys the immutability of life.

"And for the most part, these sins, so common to man, arise because of a failure to remember the reason for the existence of human life. If it is recognized that God is the *raison d'être* for everything one will make no mistake."

"Those who have missed the mark morally desire to repudiate God and His reign in order to cover up their sin. For this reason as long as there is sin in the world so long will there be atheists. Among those who seriously advocate atheism there are many for whom the existence of God would be most embarrassing. They want none of an umpireship so rigorous as His. They want to count God out and deport themselves in their own self-willed way.

"In a word, they want to be God. Setting themselves up as the criterion, they reverse the standards for right and wrong. According to their standard, everything that clashes with their wishes is evil. Everything that suits their fancy, even illicit lust and the spoliation of their fellows, is good. They have a mania for self. They are obsessed by a passion for self-aggrandizement.

"The criterion for right and wrong must be projected out of life that is eternal. It must not be cheapened and changed to suit the convenience of the individual. God is life eternal and not notional creation with which one can play fast and loose. Let the atheists indulge their mania to their heart's content. The while life ever moves solemnly forward."

"Human sorrow centers its attention on a part and fails to comprehend the whole. Those who indulge in introspection are inclined to magnify minor matters. For this reason the nerves snap.

"Men who march boldly to war and count the killing of men an honor become nervous when in a crowded place some one's toe is stepped on. A woman addicted to adultery flies into a rage over another person's failure to tell the truth. The capitalist who squeezes millions out of the working classes considers the theft of one flower vase an irreparable loss.

"We need to look at evil in its entirety. There is very deep meaning in the fact that Ishikawa, far famed as Japan's robber chief, insisted that the famous warrior-statesman, Toyotomi Hideyoshi, was a far greater robber than himself.

"Those who live in the inner chamber of introspection need constantly to take lessons in great nature's out-of-doors. Failure to do this results in many misjudgments regarding evil."

VII. Suffering

"Suffering, when it envisions a great goal, is transformed into privilege. The martyr chooses pain as the pathway to glory. The patriot thinks of the field of battle as the arena of honor. Therefore, suffering must not be set off by itself and thought of merely as suffering. It is necessary to ignore pain and look at the totality of one's mission in life!

"He who drinks but gingerly out of life's fountain will know but little about the mystery of suffering. He, however, who drinks deeply will understand that it is the very greatest of arts.

"The same can be said regarding the contradictions, errors, and evils in the world. It is most dangerous to make oneself the center in judging the total situation. We must remember that in this world there are many besides ourselves.

"Moreover, the present must not be made the basal criterion by which to judge the totality of things. There are cases where the inconsistencies of the present are in their essential nature, harmony. The fact that an infant cannot stand must not be accounted an inconsistency.

"It must be kept in mind that, as regards the world's evils, there is a masterly Providence transcending human wisdom, incessantly at work."

"I discover a multitude of things in the words of Christ, 'Except a grain of wheat fall into the ground and die it abideth by itself alone, but if it die it beareth much fruit.' Truly the mysterious meaning of eternal life is that the way to gain is to lose.

"Religion may be looked upon as a means in the economy of life by which we learn first to suffer loss in order to get great gain. Buddha preached Nirvana and taught that terrific loss leads thither. Jesus showed us the same thing in the Cross. The road of negation taught by Buddha opened the way to full affirmation in the attainment of Buddhahood. The Cross of Christ had the resurrection as its promise."

"One of Japan's literary lights teaches that we must, at any cost, be superior to our age. To this I would add, he who would know the superior way must know the way which leads to the incarnation. The Buddhist teaching points to this way. The Carpenter of Nazareth walked this way. He who was sneered at as being 'gluttonous and a winebibber' did not think of labor and religion in separate terms.

"He neither fasted nor observed the ceremonies of purification, but as a friend of sinners and an adviser of harlots He was covered with the dust and dirt of the vulgar world. Here His incarnation led Him.

"Moreover, the reason He died on the Cross as a criminal under the sentence of death was because He took this road which led downward. He who offered up His flesh as a blood-offering espoused religion in its ultimate form. When Christ uttered His last words as a criminal on the Cross, the world even to the last being in it was absorbed Godward."

VIII. Love

"Until love germinates in one's own soul it is impossible to understand the love of God. The self-willed soul takes all favors for granted. When misfortune comes it immediately becomes pessimistic and begins to curse both the world and God.

"Love wells up from within. When it does not flow forth from an inner source it can never understand the preciousness of the love of others. It is like the rich who cannot understand the hardships of the toiling poor.

"In proportion as there is love within us, in that measure will love get near to God. When we strive to live in love we immediately understand the essence of the universe. Its essence is love. This is the meaning of the words, 'He that loveth not, knoweth not God, for God is love.' "

"Love knows all things. Love knows sorrow. Love knows laughter. Love knows endurance. Love knows action. Love knows hunger. Love knows growth. Love knows adventure. Love knows reverence. Love knows pride. Love knows magnanimity. For this reason love approaches omniscience.

"Love contentedly suffers hardship. Love works miracles. This is the reason that love approaches omnipotence.

"Love is effervescent. Love saturates. Love fuses. Love embraces. Thus love is flexible and adaptable. Love is the final reality."

"In love there is unconscious love, subconscious love, and conscious love. Love as it evolves in the ovary belongs to the unconscious type.

"Affection, mother love, mutual helpfulness, racial love, belong to subconscious love. This takes the form of sacrifice and making good another's lack.

"Further, it becomes atoning love, does not begrudge the death of the Cross for unknown sinners and becomes love in its highest development. In this full-conscious love is born anew the love which purposes to make good the very last defects of the universe.

"This love causes the unconscious love in the universe to blossom out as conscious love. Through this I know that the will of the universe, even in unconsciousness, is love, in subconsciousness it is love, and in full consciousness it is love. This is my philosophy, my science, my religion."

"Some people think salvation comes through merit. To me this is unbelievable. Salvation is the unending power of the vast love of the universe. Aside from love there is no salvation. Where love exists there must be salvation. If there is love, salvation's arm cannot fail to reach out after the undeserving.

"Faith as related to salvation means a faith that love is hidden away at the heart of the universe. There is nothing strange in the fact that Buddhism recognizes the existence of this love and that Christianity discovered it. God does not make a distinction between Buddhism and Christianity. He has but one love. He includes even so unworthy a being as myself in a part of His plan. Blessed be His name."

IX. Religion

"Religion is the greatest of all the arts. What generally goes by the name of art is fragmentary and appeals only to the senses. Religion alone is an art which takes in the whole of living and is an art of life itself.

"When we live by religion we are able for the first time to sit before God's mirror. The soul functions as a medium of expression, clothing the material forms, and they in turn reveal the structure of the soul.

"Religion is the most delightful of arts. To me it is the highest of arts. There is no need of spectators. I tread its stage alone. Even when I weep shrouded in darkness God does not fail to see. On this stage God and I are the actors who enact all the scenes. Even though I be the most stupid of actors, God does not show contempt."

"It is said that in ancient Sparta they put much emphasis on using the fewest possible words to express the greatest possible meaning. It is difficult to estimate the blessing which would come to human beings if things could be carried through with simply a 'yes' or a 'no.' There is no class that uses so many superfluous words as those who live by squeezing their existence out of their fellows.

"Even among religions, the religion which exploits people uses the greatest number of words. In contrast with this the laboring class has no time for many or long words. Their words are short and to the point.

"The words of all who are in a fighting mood are short. 'Attention!' 'Forward march!' 'Halt!' These are the words of warriors. The laboring class, trained on life's rough field of battle, naturally uses the words of fighting men.

"In the realm of religion the words of militant prophets are short. As for me, let it be 'Yes, yes, no, no.' To me oft-reiterated prayers are useless."

"It is utterly impossible for me to have a sincere respect for professionalized religious leaders. Even though conferences regarding the decline of faith in doctrine and creeds be repeated a million times, if there is no deliberation as to ways and means for the actual practice of love, how will it be possible to discover a religion pulsating with life and warm as though human blood were coursing through it?

"The reason the so-called schools of religion of our day

are conferring learning on the spiritually dead is because they are absorbed in the higher criticism of doctrines and articles of faith. Doctrines and creeds are the outer garments, not the inner life. Genuine religion will, therefore, only be discovered when professional religionists are cleared out of the way and a democracy of faith is established.

"Christ was a carpenter. He was not a graduate of the Jerusalem Theological Seminary. St. Francis just missed being a jockey. He was not of the priestly line. When faith is committed to professional leaders, religion inevitably starts a downward course."

"Love toward man is not the whole of religion. The upward reach of one's soul, a mind that knows no turmoil, a spirit which is unafraid in the presence of pain, a spirit courageous in the face of death, a spirit that knows self-restraint and self-control, a spirit that does not lose its reverence even in its dreams, these to me bulk large in religion.

"Moreover, my religion takes on even larger dimensions as it faces up to the universe. For me God invades not only the whole range of human life, but also the vast unchartered frontiers which lie beyond.

"Where the form of the absolute is revealed in the finite world the religious life takes on absorbing interest. Where omnipotent power is revealed within a limited sphere the hidden significance of life gushes forth. Seen from the absolute world, our finite world is but a part of an absolute whole.

"To God all things are holy. To introduce this holy mood into the life of carnal desires is the essence of the incarnate life. With a frame of mind that is free, in reality free, to live the life of the flesh and still not be stained by its pollution, this is the forthshining of a son of God.

"In this kind of life the love-passion and purity fuse and the finite world, like the flower blossoming on the bough, becomes resplendent with glory. As the flower does not concern itself about the tip of the twig, so he who knows the hidden significance of the incarnation is not in the least tempted by a sensuously enthralled world.

"Even though betrayed by tears and death, the flower of the son of God blossoms like a sunflower in great profusion. Why is it that the reproduction process of the plants is admired and the human love-passion alone is considered indecent? For those who make God their point of departure this passion of love is as beautiful as a flower. Not only so, through the love-passion one comes in contact afresh with a light that is luminous."

"The aspiration for holiness—this is the outcome of the moral life and the very heart of religious living. When one is charmed by the Holy One and as a captive of the Holy of Holies offers himself up as a mass on God's altar, morals become a festival and religion becomes a sweet-scented perfume rising Godward.

"Holiness is the heavenward open window of the soul. Holiness is the well which God has dug deep down into a man's spirit. Eternally God looks into the soul through this open window. And sometime the day will dawn when the soul will courageously wing its way upward through this window opening toward heaven.

"There is but one straight path to holiness. There must be no winding hither and thither. This path is known only to the sanctified whose faces are set toward the supreme domain.

"Those who are led astray by low lustings perish at the very sight of the brightness of holiness's dazzling light. Holiness is the very apple of God's eye."

"God must not be thought of as an abstract thing. God is life itself. Life generates life. Man is the recipient of life and the giver of it is life itself.

"There is one thing that both those who do not take an objective view of God and those who look upon the universe as an illusion cannot deny, that is their own existence.

"We have life. I do not set up God objectively. I think of life itself as God. Life surges in upon me and moves on eternally. This eternal life is God.

"Even those who deny God's objective existence cannot deny the reality of life. Life because of its reality is absolute.

"Life in me has an end in view. It is thus personalized. Why is it strange to call this absolute life, which possesses a purpose, God? As for me, God is neither objective nor subjective, but life—absolute life."

"It is foolish to seek for God outside of oneself. This will result either in idolatry or in scepticism. To seek God within oneself is better, but there is danger lest this will result in ego-mania, in becoming an opponent of order or a nihilist.

"Therefore, he who truly seeks God should discover the unchangeable laws which operate outside of himself and recognize within himself a profound and mysterious purpose. Through being cognizant of a power which pervades both within and without, cognizant also of a world of growth which is common to both, recognizing, moreover, the immutability of the moral order and recognizing the fact that God as life fills both the inner and the outer, that He is the creator of absolute values, the preserver and unfolder of all things, thus and thus only will one be able to cease going astray."

"I walk along one straight path. I possess but one little soul. This single soul I offer up to the only God. One type of love gives birth to one type of faith. One faith gives birth to one hope.

"Without turning to the left or swerving to the right I move forward along one path. Let the wise leave the path, if they will! I, as God's fool, will be tied up to God's way. The world's wise have one or even two alternate roads. But as a road to God I find but one simple trail. This is the straight road which unites two points—God and myself. Besides this I have no road. I am not interested in circles or ellipses. As God's fool, for evermore, I will walk along the straight line which connects God and myself."

X. Miracles

"Miracles! Miracles! Life is a miracle! Death is a miracle! Law is a miracle! Reality is a miracle! Illness is a miracle! Recovery is a miracle! Everything has an existence independent of mine. This is a miracle!

"The flight of the dragonfly, the transformation of the caterpillar, the trees clothing themselves in green verdure, the bough on which the gray starling sits as it whispers to my soul, the ant wriggling in the sand,—everything is a miracle. A power greater than I rules the world. I nod approval and marvel at the ever-changing form of changeless nature."

XI. Faith

"Faith means a realization of the fact that one is loved. It means a belief that love is stronger than disease, stronger than disaster, and stronger than death. In a word, it means belief that, impotent though it seems, love is mightier than the sword.

"For this reason faith of itself avails nothing. Faith as a psychological phenomenon does not necessarily mean atoning salvation. The only power which can atone is the inherent love which runs through the whole universe. The consciousness that this power is also at work within one's own being, this is true religious faith.

"We must not think narrowly of religion. Religion must be thought of as the activity of life in its entirety, striving to vitalize this inherent love. Faith is only a valve for sending the dynamic power of love in full force into the vaporizer of the soul. Love is religion itself. Faith is its gateway."

XII. Prayer

"I am a man of prayer. Naturally, there are times when I ponder as to whether from the standpoint of philosophy it is a good or bad thing to pray. But I do not pray because it is philosophically the thing to do. I pray because I am a living being. I was made to grow. A growing being has certain requirements. I place these requirements before the Lord of life. This, to me, is prayer.

"I pray to God regarding everything. But I do not pray simply for myself. I pray for the consummation of God's work in the world. The prophet Jeremiah said that if God did not answer his prayer it would reflect on His own honor. That exactly expresses my own feelings.

"I make my requests to God. I make these requests with a great outpouring of soul. I believe that without fail God answers these prayers, for I am not praying for myself. If I do not see prayer granted I decide that God has simply postponed the project. Prayer is a potent part of my life."

XIII. The Yonder Side of Life

"Because he insisted that the problem of immortality does not have a central place in religion, a man was recently excommunicated from a religious group.

"It is unquestionably true that for him to whom life is absolute the soul's immortality is not a cardinal part of religion. He who thinks of the immortality of his own soul puts self first and God second.

"To my mind the theory of the immortality of the soul is a most egotistic doctrine. It can by no means be said to be a religious concept of the highest possible type. Rather the profound faith which declares that it will obey God whether or not there be life after death is devotion of an absolute kind.

"Still, personally I make the immortality of the soul central. It cannot be said that the religion which teaches immortality is no religion. It may not be a religion which creates values, but it certainly is a religion which conserves them. Gratitude for the joy of being preserved is undoubtedly one way of life. I want to think broadly about religion."

"To me death is purification Godward. The life after death I leave entirely to Him. I do not trouble myself much about the question as to whether the soul is mortal or immortal. If only God lives I am content to die.

"However, if it is well that one so unworthy as I should live, life will be a grateful gift. Yet if through death the impotency of my soul is laid bare, how great will be my shame before God. None the less, I believe in salvation."

"Death to me is the pathway to God. I cannot believe otherwise. Even now it is God who gives me life. If life is God's gift, is not death, which is one of the variations of life, also the work of His hand?

"If I praise God for life, can I refrain from praising Him for death? Let me in response to that solemn summoning voice quietly commit my soul to God. Death cannot be a victor over me. Through death I am a victor Godward. Nay, God is ever victorious over death. He tramples it under His feet."